THE
VICTORS
OF IMAM HUSSAIN

AYATOLLAH MUHAMMAD MAHDI
CHAMSEDDINE

THE MAINSTAY
FOUNDATION

Author: Ayatollah Muhammad Mahdi Chemseddine

Translated and Edited by: The Mainstay Foundation

© 2015 The Mainstay Foundation

Printed in the United States.

ISBN: 978-1943393084

Contents

ABOUT THE AUTHOR

Ayatollah Sheikh Muhammad Mahdi Chamseddine was a prominent Shia-Lebanese religious scholar, intellectual, and public figure. He was one of the founders of the Supreme Shia Islamic Council in Lebanon, along with Sayyid Musa Al-Sadr and others. Chamseddine and Sadr were heavily involved in preaching a moderate understanding of Islam that espoused plurality and coexistence at a time when Lebanon was going through an extreme period of violent civil war. After the disappearance of Sadr in 1978, Chamseddine rose to the forefront as his successor.

Chamseddine was not only a religious figure, but a public intellectual and political thinker. He led Lebanon in its national and political introspection, always calling for inter-faith and intra-faith dialogue. He made the unity and advancement of Lebanon his priority through his calls for civic engagement, national sovereignty, and resistance to occupation. At the same time, his theory of political legitimacy was based on notions of social contract and popular sovereignty, as opposed to other prevalent Islamist ideologies at the time. I one of his most influential books *Nidham Al-Hukm Wa Al-Idara fi Al-Islam (The System of Government and Public Administration in Islam)*, Chamseddine set out his theory of national sovereignty based on Islamic teachings that gave religious legitimacy to representative government.

Chamseddine also played a central role in the establishment of the Islamic University of Lebanon, which became a leading institution in the country, including in fields such as surveying and biomedical engineering. The University is a member of the International Association of Universities and the Francophone University Association, as well as a number of other regional associations. Chamseddine also established a number of other institutions, including schools, orphanages, and social service organizations.

Chamseddine was born in Najaf, Iraq, in 1936 to a family known for religious and scholarly achievement. His father had migrated to Najaf to pursue his religious studies there. In 1948, while Chamseddine was still 12 years old, his father decided to return to Lebanon. Chamseddine stayed in Najaf to pursue his own religious education. During his stay of over 30 years in Iraq, Chamseddine studied with the most prominent Shia religious scholars, including Grand Ayatollah Muhsen Al-Hakim, Grand Ayatollah Abulqasim Al-Khoei, and Grand Ayatollah Muhammad Al-Rouhani. He rose to prominence in Najaf and became a distinguished member of the seminary. In 1969,

Chamseddine returned to Lebanon, where he began his illustrious legacy as a public figure. He survived an assassination attempt in 1990 and passed away due to illness at age 65 in 2001.

Translator's Preface

It was a great honor to have the opportunity to translate a book for a learned scholar and Muslim thinker such as Ayatollah Chamseddine. The book provided great insight into the movement of Imam Hussain (a) and its impact in changing history. May his soul rest in peace alongside the heroes who he dedicated his life to learn and write about.

Before our readers begin on the journey of this book, we hope that they keep a few important points in mind.

Firstly, there are great structural differences between the original Arabic language of the book and the modern English language. Such structural differences make the task of literal translation burdensome, and creates a final result that does not accurately capture the spirit and readability of the Arabic text. Because Ayatollah Chamseddine's work could not be encapsulated in a direct or literal translation, our translation method had to be oblique. Adaptations were used freely to capture the meaning of the text without being bogged down in the structural differences of the two languages.

The process of translation always begs us to find precise meanings for the passages that we translate. But when we encounter the majesty of the Holy Quran, we find ourselves incapable of understanding its intricacies, let alone translating its true and deep meanings. We turned to the works of translators who have attempted to do this before. Although no translation can do justice to the Holy Quran, we found that the translation of Ali Quli Qarai to be the most proper in understanding when compared to the interpretation of the text as derived by our grand scholars. As such, we decided to rely on Qarai's translations throughout this book, with minor adaptations that allowed us to weave the verses more properly with the rest of the work.

A second great limitation came with translating the narrations of the Grand Prophet Muhammad (s) and his Holy Household (a). Their words are ever so deep and ever so powerful. We attempted to convey these passages to the reader in a tone that is understandable without deviating from the essence of the words of these immaculate personalities. We pray that we were successful in this endeavor.

Finally, we want to take this opportunity to thank you for your support. As students of Islam and as translators of this text, our greatest purpose is to please God by passing along these teachings to others. By picking up this book, you have lent your crucial support to this endeavor. We hope that you will continue your support throughout the rest of this book, and we ask that you keep us in your prayers whenever you pick it up.

The Editorial and Translation Team,

The Mainstay Foundation

INTRODUCTION

In the Name of God, the Beneficent, the Merciful

All praise belongs to God, Lord of All Worlds. May God shower peace and blessings upon His Messenger, Muhammad, and Muhammad's pure progeny.

There is one dimension among the dimensions of Imam Hussain's revolution that has not yet been studied at all. That dimension is the in-depth human dimension.

In the course of my research, it has become clear to me that this dimension is one of deep valleys, wide expanses, and broad horizons.

I cannot say that what I have written has penetrated to all of its depths and extended to the broadest of its horizons. For such an aspiration would require a careful and patient study, relying on all reachable sources, perhaps even some sources untraditional to the likes of these studies, such as books on genealogy. Furthermore, such an aspiration would require one to examine the relationships between the two predominant groups of clans:

the Arabs of the North, and the Arabs of the South. Then one would need to examine the relationships between clans within each of these two groups. Next, one would need to examine the connections between the divisions and subdivisions of each clan as well as their internal relationships. The following step would be to connect all of that to the geographical locations of these clans in Iraq, Hijaz, Syria, and perhaps, in the greater sphere, to Egypt and North Africa.

Moreover, such an aspiration would require a more extensive and comprehensive study of the positions taken by the non-Arab Muslims in that early era. The conclusion I reach here is that the non-Arab Muslims did not have a role in this revolution. While I am confident regarding the truth of this conclusion, there is another important question to be addressed: To what extent did this revolution contribute to awakening the non-Arab Muslims to their own significance, the oppression that had befallen them, and their ability to bring about change?

One would also have to address many other important matters, such as: To which extent was the cohesiveness of the clan-based structure maintained in Islamic society at the time? What was the true, covert position of the Abbasids toward the Alids in the midst of the political and revolutionary activity that intensified in the last third of the first century and the beginnings of the second century after the Hijrah? Before eliminating the Umayyads and after establishing the Abbasid state, there existed those of deviant and whimsical schools of thought. These individuals were either from non-Islamic groups or from groups that hid behind the garb of Islam. What was the truth behind the relationship of the Abbasids and their preachers with these types of individuals? There are also other questions.

The answers provided in this study to some of these issues and to other issues, which I have not mentioned in this foreword, are insufficient. While this does not mean that they are incorrect, they, nonetheless, require further elaboration.

* * *

I began writing this study in order for it to be an appendix to the third edition of my book, *Thawrat al-Hussain: Durufuha al-'Ijtima'iyyah wa 'Atharuha al-'Insaniyyah.* However, the issues that this study raised would draw me in to expand on them. The result was the chapters before you, which are greater than to be an appendix to a book. Hence, I decided to publish these chapters in a separate book.

This study consists of three parts:

1. Introductions: Regarding the dimensions of the idea and its objectives, as well as the sources cited in the study.

2. How many are they and who are they? Regarding the martyrs of Imam Hussain's revolution – the Hashimids and others in Karbala and Kufa. This includes a description of each of them within the limitations of the information available about each of them. There is also

an appendix in which I include the text of the ziyarah (visit salutation) attributed to al-Nahiyah al-Muqaddasah as well as al-Ziyarah al-Rajabiyyah (visit salutation of Rajab). Moreover, there is also an important chapter investigating the status of these two ziyarahs due to them being sources cited in this study. In that chapter, I favor reliance on the ziyarah attributed to al-Nahiyah and consider al-Ziyarah al-Rajabiyyah to be a secondary, unimportant source.

3. Implications that can be concluded from the information relating to these personalities, the condition of the state and society, and the circumstances leading up to, during and following the battle.

* * *

It appears to me that this study represents a novel method in dealing with and understanding historical texts, especially regarding that which is related to the study of revolutions and the masses behind those revolutions in Islamic history. For, indeed, the history of revolutions has been subject to destruction and distortion by the narrators and historians who would fawn over or fear the authorities. Hence, the task of a historian is very difficult in this field. It may be that this is the best of way allowing a researcher to reach a great extent of the truth.

* * *

If this study – with the approach it was founded upon and the issues it brought up, regardless whether it addressed them or was not successful in addressing them – is able to instill a desire to further search for the truth, then it would have led to the greatest of its objectives.

I ask God Almighty to make this study a deed He accepts and benefits others through. All praise belongs to God, Lord of all worlds.

Muhammad Mahdi Chamseddine

21 Jamadi al-Awwal 1394 AH

11 June 1974 CE

PROLOGUE

THE HUMAN DIMENSION

Among the dimensions of Imam Hussain's revolution that have not been studied is its "human dimension," if you will. By "human dimension" I mean that which is related to the men who fanned its flames and were martyred in its midst. I am not referring to their belief in and sincerity to the revolution. For they made that clear through their demise. Rather, I am referring to their clan-based affiliation, their human factor, their geographical backgrounds, their social status, their ages, and other matters that are relevant to the personal status of each of those individuals.

This study also covers the revolutionaries or the masses supporting the revolution who – for one reason or another – missed the opportunity to participate in the revolution when it took place, albeit while remaining loyal to it.

Studying this dimension of Imam Hussain's revolution is necessary to achieve two objectives:

First: Knowing the "degree" that the "revolutionary state" in Islamic society at the time had reached. That is from the aspect of its depth and authenticity as well as its propagation.

Second: Knowing the extent to which the martyrdom of the revolutionaries in Karbala' and elsewhere contributed to fanning the flames of the revolutions that later broke out. This is from the aspect that a revolutionary's clan-based or regional affiliations would cause his martyrdom to make some sort of change in the loyalty of some individuals and groups to the authorities. In doing so, such individuals and groups either would come into the revolutionary atmosphere or would at least stand on the sidelines.

In my book, *Thawrat al-Hussain: Durufuha al-'Ijtima'iyyah wa 'Atharuha al-'Insaniyyah*, I examined the impact of Imam Hussain's Revolution on the break out of the revolutions that followed it. I studied this from the aspect that the revolution impacted the greater community's mentality, in general, as a new cultural factor to enter the greater community's realm of ideas. I did not, however, study the direct impact of the revolution through its revolutionary personalities, their affiliations, and their places in the lives of their clan-based societies and geographical locations.

When these men are studied this way, they will be windows through which one can peek into their society and thus come to know much of that society's hidden truths. Direct quotations from historical texts do not reveal such hidden truths.

* * *

However, the core content for this type of study is almost completely absent. For, indeed, narrators of tradition and historians have not been concerned with relaying and recording the names of the men, women and groups that participated in this revolution in one way or another. They have not discussed those who attempted to participate in the revolution but who were prevented by the circumstances. They have not discussed their clans, their geographic locations and their ages. There is barely any valuable information available about the social environments that many or most of those revolutionaries came from.

One faces this information deficiency when it comes to the non-Hashimid martyrs. As for the Hashimids, historians have recorded the names of their martyrs, albeit with disagreement on some of their names. In any case, however, the situation one faces regarding the Hashimid martyrs is better than the situation one faces with the non-Hashimid martyrs.

Perhaps it is the shining light emanating from the personality of Imam Hussain and the prominent shadow of his grand personality in the soul of a researcher that are responsible – to some extent – for the negligence of the historians and narrators of tradition. That may be behind their negligence to provide the core content for this study in a better way.

Hence, attempting to gather the core content for this study faces many difficulties. The rise of these difficulties spans from a scarcity of information, to the dispersion and ambiguity of information at times, and to the contradiction of information at yet other times. Therefore, I must have a word to say about the references.

RESOURCES

The sources that can viably provide the content for this study are:

Books on Narrators. These are books describing the degree of trustworthiness, or the lack thereof, of the narrators who relay traditions. Scholars of this science of narrators have taken care to mention those martyrs. Perhaps they have done so because of the great meaningful focal point that such martyrs hold in the Islamic mindset. It is a mindset that developed as a result of their martyrdom for the sake of truth. Otherwise, most of these martyrs have not been mentioned as narrators in a chain of narrators for any tradition.

Books of History. These books are referenced because they intentionally mention some of the martyrs. This happens either because the mentioned martyr has a special place or as a presentation of the martyr through describing an event or portraying a particular situation. Furthermore, these books are a primary source for the events connected related to those martyrs and their adversaries.

Books on the Maqtal.[1] These are books that scholars or those well-versed in literature from the Twelver Shia school have written. Typically, they only narrate the history of Imam Hussain's revolution and its surrounding circumstances, from beginning to end.

Early Books of Literature. It seems that these books are of secondary value, at least as far as this particular stage of study is concerned.

* * *

As for the Books on Narrators, I will rely on the following books:

1. *Kitab al-Rijal* - by Muhammad ibn 'Abd al-'Aziz al-Kashi - deceased in the second half of the fourth century AH – (Publications of the 'A'lami Foundation for printed materials – Karbala', Iraq / Undated).

2. *Kitab al-Rijal* – by Abu al-'Abbas, 'Ahmad ibn 'Ali ibn 'Ahmad ibn al-'Abbas al-Najashi – deceased in 405 AH (Nashr Kitab Center – Mustafawi Press – Tehran / Undated).

3. *Kitab al-Rijal* – by Shaykh Muhammad ibn al-Hasan al-Tusi – deceased in 460 AH. Investigation and commentary by Sayyid Muhammad Sadiq Bahr al-

'Ulum (Al-Haydariyyah Press – Najaf : 1381 AH, 1961 CE).

4. *Mu'jam Rijal al-Hadith wa Tafsil Tabaqat al-Ruwah*, by my esteemed teacher Sayyid Abu al-Qasim al-Khoei. This is one of the most contemporary and comprehensive books written in the Science of Narrators. I have nine volumes of this book. The ninth volume was printed on the nineteenth of Rabi' al-Thani, 1394 AH at Al-'Adab Press in the holy city of Najaf.

* * *

As for the books on history, I will rely primarily on Muhammadibn Jarir al-Tabari's book *Tarikh al-Rusul wa al-Muluk* – the Dar al-Kutub edition – investigated by Muhammad Abu al-Fadl 'Ibrahim (the fifth volume, printed in 1963 CE). I chose this book as opposed to other encyclopedias because it gives a researcher the opportunity to know each report's chain of transmission and verify that it is an eyewitness report. It also gives a researcher the opportunity to compare the often several reports on a single event and favor certain reports over others.

There is no doubt that referring to other sources will be necessary in order to compare certain information and increase verification. For comparison and verification I will refer to the following books:

1. *Al-'Akhbar al-Tiwal* by Abu Hanifah al-Daynawari – deceased in 282 AH – investigated by 'Abd al-Mun'im

'Amir – the Turathuna series, published by the ministry of education and nationalistic guidance, 1960 CE.

2. *Tarikh al-Ya'qubi* by 'Ahmadibn 'Abi Ya'qub, deceased in 292 AH. Publications of Al-Haydariyyah library and press in the holy city of Najaf, 1384 AH (1964 CE).

3. *Muruj al-Dhahab wa Ma'adin al-Jawhar* by Abu al-Hasan 'Ali ibn Hussain al-Mas'udi, deceased in 346 AH – investigated by Muhammad Muhyi al-Din 'Abd al-Hamid – al-Sa'adah press in Egypt – second edition, 1367 AH (1948 CE).

In rare cases, I may have referred to the third volume of the history book by 'Ibn al-'Athir al-Jazari, *al-Kamil fi al-Tarikh*, published by Dar al-Kitab al-'Arabi – Beirut – second edition, 1387 AH (1967 CE). Moreover, at some points during the research it may have been necessary to refer to some books of literature concerning some of the individuals or events.

* * *

As for the Books on the Maqtal, I will rely on the following books:

1. *Al-'Irshad* by Shaykh al-Mufid, Muhammadibn Muhammadibn al-Nu'man, deceased in 413 AH – publications of the al-Haydariyyah press and library in the holy city of Najaf, 1381 AH (1962 CE).

2. *Maqtal Al-Hussain* by Abu al-Mu'ayyad al-Muwaffaq ibn 'Ahmad al-Makki, the greatest orator of Khuwarizm, deceased in 568 AH (the first and second volumes), al-Zahra' Press in the holy city of Najaf, 1367 AH (1948 CE).

In this book, al-Khuwarizmi relays his reports mostly from the history written by 'Ibn 'A'tham, Abu Muhammad 'Ahmad, deceased in 314 AH. Hence, these reports are at the level of al-Tabari's reports. Furthermore, his reports are generally characterized by objectivity and precise language. Moreover, these reports maintain a moderate content of emotion.

3. *Maqatil al-Talibiyyin* by Abu al-Faraj al-'Asfahani, 'Ali ibn Hussain ibn Muhammad al-Qurashi al-'Umawi al-Marwani, deceased in 356 AH, expounded and investigated by Sayyid 'Ahmad Saqr – Cairo – Dar 'Ihya' al-Kutub al-'Arabiyyah.

4. *Manaqib 'Al 'Abi Talib* by Muhammadibn 'Ali ibn Shahr 'Ashub al-Sarawi al-Mazandarani, deceased in 588 AH, (fourth volume) al-'Ilmiyyah Press – Qum, Iran – undated.

5. *Muthir al-'Ahzan* by Shaykh Najm al-Din Muhammadibn Ja'far ('Ibn Nama) al-Hilli, deceased in 645 AH – publications of the al-Haydariyyah Press in Najaf – 1369 AH (1950 CE).

6. *Al-Luhuf Fi Qatl al-Tufuf* by 'Ali ibn Musa ibn Mu-
    hammad ibn Tawous, deceased in 664 AH – publica-
    tions of the al-Haydariyyah Library and Press in Najaf
    / undated.

7. *Bihar al-'Anwar* by Shaykh al-'Islam Muhammad
    Baqir al-Majlisi, deceased in 1111 AH (Volumes 44 &
    45) from the new edition – al-Islamiyyah Press, 1385,
    publications of al-Maktabah al-'Islamiyyah in Tehran,
    Iran.

I relied on this book because it relays texts from earlier authors
of Books on the Maqtal.

8. *A ziyarah of Imam Hussain* that is attributed to the
    Twelfth Imam from Ahl al-Bayt. This ziyarah includes
    the names of many of the martyrs, both Hashimids and
    others. Al-Majlisi relayed this ziyarah in *Bihar al-
    'Anwar* (Volume 45, pages 65-73) from the book *al-
    'Iqbal* by Sayyid 'Ibn Tawus. He mentioned that it was
    introduced in the year 252 AH.

I doubt that this ziyarah is attributed to the Twelfth Imam.
Nonetheless, it is still an early historical document that can be
relied upon from a historical perspective. I will refer to it
throughout the study with the word, "Al-Ziyarah" (or "*the
ziyarah*").

9. *A ziyarah of Imam Hussain* mentioned by Sayyid Ibn
    Tawus in his book, *al-'Iqbal*, to have included a ziyarah

of the martyrs mentioning their names. It seems that this ziyarah was composed by Sayyid 'Ibn Tawus. Al-Majlisi mentioned it in *Bihar al-'Anwar* (Volume 101, pages 340-341).

I will refer to it throughout the study with the word, "Al-Rajabiyyah" (or "the ziyarah of Rajab") because it was reported in order for one to visit Imam Hussain and the martyrs with it on the first day of the month of Rajab. As a historical document, this has less value than the previous ziyarah because the previous ziyarah precedes Ibn Tawous by four centuries or more (Ibn Tawous passed away in 664 AH). Moreover, the two ziyarahs differ in some of the names. I will include the text of the two ziyarahs at the end of this book, with an explanation of the places in which they differ and a thorough study of the two.

> 10. *A'yan al-Shia* (Volume 4, Part 1) by Sayyid Muhsin al-'Amin – third edition – al-'Insaf Press, Beirut, 1380 AH – 1960 CE.

It is also worthy of recognition that Sayyid Muhsin al-'Amin is the only author in the subject at hand that has probed the names of the martyrs, both Hashimids and others, and listed their names on pages 135-138 of the aforementioned part. However, in my opinion, his work is not beyond the criticism of falling prey to the distortion of scribes. For instance, he mentioned the names of some who were not killed in the battle. In this study, I will include what he mentioned in *'A'yan al-Shia* along with my comments on it.

There are also other books on the Maqtal that I came across through the aforementioned book, *Bihar al-'Anwar*.

THE MAQTAL

Here I must say something about books on the *Maqtal*.

I find that most of these books are more worthy of being references for Imam Hussain's revolution than general history books are.

That is because, from one aspect, they are specific to telling the events of this revolution. Hence, they are more bustling with the revolution's events and details than general history books are. For, indeed, general history books most often give equal importance to everything they narrate.

From another aspect, individuals who regard Imam Hussain's revolution with a sense of love and holiness are the ones who write these books on the Maqtal. These books are a living part of their history. In telling the events of the revolution, they rely on sources that have close ties to the revolution (the Imams of Ahl al-Bayt, the men and women who accompanied the revolution from its beginning to its end in Karbala'). Narrators of general history did not contact those individuals. Narrators of general history were most often connected to the political ruler who would prevent them from relying on such individuals in their reports. At the very least, their connection with the ruler would make them beware of reporting the events as described by the women, children and companions of the revolutionaries.

Furthermore, the authors of general history books were most often either connected to the political ruler or supportive of a political condition that was at odds with the heart of the revolution. In one way or another, such authors may have come to terms with the situation of those who acted to suppress the revolution. So, naturally, they were not able to – or did not want to – record events from the perspective of such sources as the revolutionaries themselves. Those are the sources that some narrators among the Shia connected to. Men and women, their Shiasm drove them to go after every precise detail and every major event connected to the revolutionaries and their accomplishment in Karbala'. Even so, I come forward to say that even those narrators did not report everything that took place. Indeed, so much was lost and so much was effaced.

One example of that can be found in the tradition of 'Ammar al-Duhni[1] on behalf of Imam al-Baqir (Abu Ja'far, Muhammadibn 'Aliibn Hussain), cited by al-Tabari. For I believe that 'Ammar or the narrators who followed him played with this tradition, adding some ideas that pleased the authorities. (For example, the idea that during Imam Hussain's negotiations with 'Umar ibn Sa'd, Imam Hussain requested that 'Umar send him to Yazidibn Muawiyah, allowing them to shake hands and have Yazid decide what to do with him.) They also removed parts of it and abbreviated some of the key features in it. Moreover, it is not far fetched that al-Tabari himself was lenient in citing some of its parts.[2]

For these reasons, I consider books on the Maqtal worthier to be relied on than general history books when it comes to the personal history of the revolutionaries. Rather, and for the same reasons, they are worthier to be relied on than general history books when it comes to the very history of the revolution.

Admittedly, there is criticism directed at many books on the Maqtal – criticism related to the events. For, indeed, in some cases zeal and love can drive a person to include certain reports without first giving them their due diligence of investigation. Some of these reports may even be merely personal conclusions and opinions formulated by some narrators and authors. A later author would then come along and consider such conclusions to be history, recording them as events that actually occurred. Furthermore, in certain cases, some authors of books on the Maqtal project their own view of the event and thus describe it using particular attributes to describe the revolutionaries or enemies of the revolution. They also describe the entire event in emotional terms. This phenomenon exists predominantly in the works of more recent authors of books on the Maqtal.

In any case, a researcher must commit to a strictly scientific methodology in critiquing and adopting opinions.

However, in all fairness, I must say that the other historical sources (besides books on the Maqtal), which have been written by non-Shia authors about the history of this revolution, do not escape grave criticisms either.

For when one regards that which relates to the revolutionaries, one notices that the narrators and authors did not exhibit special attention to them. They did not mention any of them with the intent to mention them. Rather, they mentioned those whose names one comes across listed in the reports that they relay.

As for that which relates to the events of the revolution, one notices that in many cases they do not exhibit precision and elaboration in their relaying of its events (with the exception of Abu Mikhnaf). Some may argue that they simply dealt with the revolution like any other event from that time period. Perhaps this notion is true, but they knew and felt that this revolution was not like any other event in that time period. For it was a major sign of a major change in the Muslims' lives. This revolution was an entirely new turning point in their lives. Because of this, those historians should have flocked to relay it more than they relayed other events. They should not have missed recording anything closely or remotely related to it.

Nonetheless, I cannot accept the notion that they treated it just like any other historical event. Rather, I find that they treated it with an even lesser degree of care. They were influenced by the political direction that did not encourage relaying the events of the revolution. Rather, it was a political direction bent on covering up those events in order to keep society from being moved by them and lead to a change in some political positions.

When it comes to the Umayyads, this matter is clear. Moreover, I find it to be so even when it comes to the Abbasids.

The Abbasids considered the revolution one of their historical achievements, as they were Hashimids (note that none of the Abbasids were part of the revolution). The Abbasids also knew that they owed the revolution so much in terms of the circumstances and factors which brought them to power. Rather, the soul, slogans, and memories of that revolution were among the direct factors for their rise to power. Even so, I find that they had a negative stance toward the revolution. This is because they knew that its memories and intimations could be a threat to them from the aspect of people's view toward the legitimacy of their rise to power. For the revolution calls for turning over the reins of power to the Alids of the Hashimids. The reasons for the Abbasids' wariness toward Imam Hussain's revolution become clearer once one notices that the Hasanid revolutionary movements did not stop after the Abbasid state stabilized.

* * *

It was necessary to give this word about the books of the Maqtal in order to clarify whether or not they can be adequately used as historical references when studying this revolution. This brief word does not suffice the care that is actually required for this topic, as the books of the Maqtal can be the subject of a deep and comprehensive methodical study that looks into the development of this documentation of history – as well as its evolution, methodology, content, authors, styles of writing, evolution of style, literary context, comparative study across languages (Arabic, Farsi, Turkish, Urdu, and others), the poetic content of such books (which, we theorize, started with Abu Mikhnaf but has not yet ceased). Writing about the Maqtal – the murder of Hussain – was, and remains, a sought-after endeavor for many. Whoever embarks on such a study will thus find rich, plentiful, and diverse resources – stretching through all Muslim eras and dispersed throughout all Muslim groups and communities from the first century AH to our current fourteenth century AH.

Such a study will not be limited to the books that were authored about the tragedy of Hussain – albeit such books are the most numerous and diverse. But there are other books of this type, as many authors wrote about 'The Maqtal of Ali,' 'The Maqtal of Zayd,' 'The Maqtal of Othman,' 'The Maqtal of Hijr ibn Adi,' and others. The researcher will find tens of books of Maqtal with differing subjects. These writings, alongside the books of narration and tradition, may prove to be a significant phase in the development of historical documentation for Muslim authors.

THE MEN

HOW MANY ARE THEY?
AND WHO ARE THEY?

THE STANCE

During his stay in Mecca a group from the people of Hijaz and a group from the people of Basra joined Imam Hussain's (a) family and followers.[1] Al-Khawarizmi specifies the number of people that joined Imam Hussain (a) from Mecca:

> ... *He left Mecca on a Tuesday, the Day of Tarwiya, with eight days having passed from Dhil-Hijja. With him were eighty-two men of his followers and family members.*[2]

It is possible that this number that Al-Khawarizmi narrates is not accurate in regards to the number. And in any case we don't have a correct estimate for the statistics of all his followers and supporters when he left Mecca.

Abu Mikhnif said,

> ... *When Hussain left Mecca he was intercepted by the messengers of Amr ibn Saeed ibn Al-Aass, with Yahya ibn Saeed leading them. They said, 'Where do you think you're going?!' He ignored them and moved forward. The*

two groups stood before one another. Amr's messengers pulled out their whips but Hussain and his companions would firmly stand their ground. Hussain continued on his path.[3]

Al-Daynouri said,

… And when Hussain was intercepted by Amr ibn Saeed ibn Al-Aass' police chief along with a group of soldiers, the police chief said, 'The Prince orders you to leave your journey, so leave. And if you do not I will stop you from going.' So he and his soldiers stood in Hussain's way. The confrontation grew. The soldiers took out their whips. Amr ibn Saeed was informed of the situation. He feared that it would get out of hand so he gave the police chief word to let them pass.[4]

Therefore, there were official attempts, characteristic of violence and aggression, to halt Imam Hussain (a) from leaving Mecca. However, those attempts failed.[5]

Abu Mikhnif said,

Hussain did not go through any village except that they followed him. When he was arrived at a village called Zubala he received the news of the murder of Abdullah ibn Baqtur, his foster brother. Muslim ibn Aqeel was also killed. The news of his murder came to Hussain during his stay in Zubala. At this point he went before the people and read the following:

'In the Name of God the Beneficent the Merciful. I have received tragic news. Muslim ibn Aqeel, Hani ibn Urwa, and Abdullah ibn Baqtur were all murdered. We have been abandoned by our followers. Whoever of you wishes to leave now will not be blamed.'

People began to disperse, left and right, until only those who came with him from Mecca remained.[6] He did this because he feared that those who had followed his caravan thought that he was headed to a land where he will become the certain ruler. He hated that they would follow him without knowing what they were truly headed to. He knew that if he delivered to them this news, only those who were most loyal and wished to die alongside him would remain.[7]

Al-Daynouri said,

He was joined by people from the homes along the road… when they heard the news of Muslim, thinking that he would arrive with victors and supporters, they left him and only the closest to him remained.[8]

Thus, only the true revolutionaries stayed after their fate was revealed and their stance was made clear.

The announcement that Imam Hussain (a) gave in Zubala was the first test for the people with him on his journey. The consequence of it was the loss of many who had joined his caravan as opportunists. The few men that stood firmly beside Hussain (a) would become known by history as the *Victors of Hussain*.

They would be tested again on the 10th night of Muharram, when Imam Hussain (a) told them to save themselves and leave.

> *The night has shrouded you, so ride into the night. Let each one of you take a member of my household [as a guardian] and disperse in the lands and cities. May God reward you all. These people ask for me, not for you... and if they get to me they will be too preoccupied to go after anyone else.*[9]

They refused this gesture. They promised to stay with him until the very end. They fought valiantly and were martyred all together.

We will see that none of the companions that joined the Imam (a) from Mecca remained, given the small number of men that joined him and committed thereafter to their honorable fate.

How Many Were They?

Surely we won't be able to determine the exact number of the companions of Imam Hussain (a), who was martyred and wasn't, because the direct evidence for this issue – the narrations of eyewitnesses – have differing views. And naturally it was not built on statistics; rather, these views were based on witnessing with the naked eye and providing rough estimations, as that was the reasonable method offered in such circumstances. Thus, any number provided does not represent an exact total but instead is an approximation that can be more or less the actual number of companions present on that day.

Here we will showcase some primary narrations on this issue, analyze them and discuss them.

* * *

We have four narrations in regards to those who participated in the battle from the Hashimites and the non-Hashimites.

1. Narration of Al-Mas'oudi

> *When Hussain reached Al-Qadisiya he was met by Al-Hur ibn Yazid Al-Tamimi... he turned and moved toward Karbala, with him were five hundred cavalry from his family members and companions and around one hundred infantry.[1]*

Al-Mas'oudi did not mention his reference in this narration. Even though Al-Mas'oudi is known for his meticulousness in his historical discourse, we cannot accept the number he provides in this narration describing the number of companions with Imam Hussain (a) arriving in Karbala. This narration contradicts all of the known narrations on this subject – ones that have provided references – without standing out as superior to the others so that we can ignore the rest and use Al-Mas'oudi's.

This narration could be correct to an extent if we were to remove its geographical context and gave it an earlier time – before Imam Hussain (a) was met by Al-Hur near Karbala. The narration could be correct if it were referring to the period of time before Imam Hussain's (a) announcement of the murders of Muslim ibn Aqeel, Abdullah ibn Baqtur, and Hani ibn Urwa. Any time after that would definitely show that the companions with Imam Hussain (a) were much less than the number provided by Al-Mas'oudi.

2. Narration of Ammar Al-Duhani

Ammar Al-Duhani narrates from Abu Ja'far, Imam Muhammad Al-Baqir (a):

When there was about three miles[2] between him and Al-Qadisiya, Al-Hur ibn Yazeed Al-Tamimi met him… so he went down and set camp. With him were forty-five cavalry and one hundred infantry.[3]

Ibn Nama Al-Hilli mentions this same number but differs on the account of timing. Ammar Al-Duhani's narration is in the context of Imam Hussain's (a) first hour of arrival in Karbala – being the 2nd of Muharram.[4] Ibn Nama gives this number but on the 10th of Muharram during the mobilization of the Imam's (a) forces. "… And Hussain mobilized his companions – they were forty-five cavalry and one hundred infantry."[5] The same was narrated by Ibn Tawous.

Note that Ammar Al-Duhani references Imam Al-Baqir (a) as his source.[6] Most probably not having any other sources, Ibn Nama – just like Ibn Tawous – relied on the narration by Ammar Al-Duhani. The reason for the difference in regards to the context of time from Ammar's narration is their lack of prudence or precision in studying and relating his narration.

Ammar Al-Duhani received his narration from the most trusted sources – Imam Al-Baqir (a) – which would necessitate an illustration of a clear, almost live, picture of what took place. Ammar asked for the narration by saying to the Imam (a), "Tell me the saga of Hussain in a way that I can relive it…" Thus, it's quite surprising at times to see these deviations from the narrations that provide the details directly from the source – the Imam (a) himself – on the accurate historical context and what actually happened in Karbala. We postulate that this caused by the fabrication of the narrators as we discussed previously. Nonetheless, this doesn't mean we can't accept the number used in the narration on a preliminary level.

Finally, we note that the narration by Ammar corresponds, both in time and place, with the first narration we mentioned previously by Al-Mas'oudi.

3. NARRATION OF AL-HUSSEYN IBN ABDEL-RAHMAN

Husseyn ibn Abdel-Rahman relates from Saad ibn Ubayda,

> *Men from the people of Kufa stood on a hill [watching the battle] and cried, 'God bring forth your victory!' I said, 'O enemies of God, why don't you go down there and aid him [i.e. Imam Hussain]?' Then Hussain came forward to speak to the messenger of Ibn Ziyad. I looked at him and noticed he was wearing a thick rigid overcoat. They spoke briefly and he left. As he left a man from the Tamim tribe by the name of Umar Al-Tahwee launched an arrow at him. I saw the arrow land between his shoulders and through his overcoat... When they rejected [his overtures to avoid the bloodshed] he had returned to his camp. I looked at their ranks. They were about a hundred men. Amongst them were five sons of Ali ibn Abi Talib, sixteen from the tribe of Hashim, an ally from the tribe of Saleem, an ally from the tribe of Kinana, and Ibn Umar ibn Ziyad.*[78]

This narration is related from an eye witness – Saad ibn Ubayda – who seemed to be with Umar ibn Saad and close to him even. He says in another narration, "We are [mired in a swamp] alongside Umar ibn Saad."[9] At the same time the narration above indicates that he was empathetic to Imam Hussain (a) and his movement where he said, "I said, 'O enemies of God, why don't you go down there and aid him [i.e. Imam Hussain]?'"[10]

The narration – with regards to the numbers it mentions – is generally aligned with the more specific narration by Al-Khawarizmi that said Imam Hussain (a) left Mecca with eighty-two men. Al-Khawarizmi repeated the number in a discrediting manner however saying, '… just as this number was cited in other sources that we have not directly reviewed," in his discussion on the 10th day of Muharram.

It seems that this narration – with regards to the time and place – illustrated the positions on the 10th of Muharram before the battle took place. Perhaps it illustrated what took place before the battle was commenced – after the first offensive for example. The illustration of Umar Al-Tahwee launching an arrow at Imam Hussain (a) after he turned around to go back to his camp, however, is not mentioned in the other narrations that relate the speeches and words of the Imam (a) with the Umayyad army. The same can be said about the people in the narration that were crying and praying to God to bring His victory to the Imam (a) while they stood and watched.

4. NARRATION OF ABU MIKHNIF

Abu Mikhnif relates from Al-Dhahhak ibn Abdullah Al-Mashriqi,

> *... And when Umar ibn Saad prayed the noon prayers... and that day was the day of Ashura, he went out with whoever was with him of people... and Hussain mobilized his companions and led them in prayer – with him were thirty-two cavalry and forty infantry.*[11]

Abu Mikhnif enjoys a solid a reputation given his precision and honesty in reporting historical traditions. He reported this narration by means of one of the companions of Imam Hussain (a) that fought alongside him – of the two that remained – and here it is Al-Dhahhak ibn Abdullah Al-Mashriqi. Al-Dhahhak, as it has come to be seen, was a firm, practicing, and meticulous man. When Imam Hussain (a) requested that he join him as one of his supporters, he accepted with the condition that he would be given leave when he saw that his fighting would no longer be of any benefit to defending the Imam (a). Imam Hussain (a) accepted his condition and Al-Dhahhak earnestly joined the fight. This particular note points to his diligence and meticulous nature.

This narration – with regards to number, time, and place – agrees with the narrations by Al-Tabari's contemporaries or those who preceded him. Amongst them is Abu Haneefa Al-Daynouri who narrates, "... Hussain (a) mobilized his companions as well, who were thirty-two cavalry and forty infantry."[12]

Al-Daynouri references a source other than the one used by Abu Mikhnif in his narration above. Another narrator in this regard is Al-Ya'qoubi. "… And Hussain had sixty-two or seventy-two men from his family and companions," he states.[13]

Also, narrations by later writers agree with this number – the most significant amongst them in our view being Al-Khawarizmi. He said, "In the morning, Hussain (a) mobilized his companions and had with thirty-two cavalry and forty infantry."[14] In addition, to these narrators Shaykh Al-Mufeed is also included amongst them. [15]

* * *

These are the primary narrations in this discussion.

We observe that, before we mention our own evaluation in this issue, the number of the Imam's (a) companions was not fixed throughout the stages of his journey. From the time he left Mecca to the afternoon of the 10th of Muharram in Karbala, the numbers changed. When he left Mecca the number started out with what Al-Khawarizmi mentioned (eighty-two men) and then increased on the road to Iraq. Then it decreased and dwindled down to the original number, and perhaps decreased beyond that. Then the number once again increased, but only nominally, right before or when the battle with some supporters coming forth. This was in addition to some of the Umayyad soldiers abandoning their posts and joining the camp of Imam Hussain (a).

Our own particular assessment at the end of this study is that the number of companions that were martyred with Imam Hussain (a) in Karbala, including Arabs and non-Arabs, come out to be approximately a hundred men or perhaps a bit more.[16]

We are unable to pinpoint an exact number because undoubtedly there are possibilities of typographical errors in the names and the lack of precision on the part of narrators who related the course of events and the actual names of the companions. Nonetheless, the margin of error here is not a significant one.

The conclusion here is in agreement with the vast majority of the narrations that illustrate what took place in the first offensive of the battle of Karbala.

Al-Khawarizmi says in his narration relating from Abu Mikhnif,

> ... and when the first offensive took place, the companions of Hussain (a) were lessened and those that remained are those mentioned in the duels that took place thereafter. A little more than fifty men were killed.[17]

Ibn Shahr Ashoub mentions that they were about forty men that were martyred in the first offensive.[18] So if we add to this number the total number of companions that were mentioned in the duels – approximately forty men – we would have gotten closer to the conclusion that we have come to from this study.

Here it is important to realize that the discrepancy in numbers between the narrators is both acceptable and reasonable. This is simply, as mentioned previously, because the narrators in all of their narrations on the number of Imam Hussain's (a) companions did not use statistics. They utilized the widely used method of approximation by mere eyesight. It is also important to acknowledge that the number of this small force could have been counted differently given that some of the supporters – the servants particularly – could appear and disappear due to special assignments.

If we took all of these into consideration, we will see that the conclusion of this study in regards to the number of non-Hashimite companions is quite meticulous and precise.

Finally, before moving forward from this point to the next part of the discussion, we note that the situation is complete. It is more probable that all of the men were martyred. Still, the eyewitnesses describe the situation on its way to completion. Some of the companions were still alive at the time the narration illustrates the scene. Thus, it leads us to assume that some of them, by way of some of the narrations, were not martyred.

* * *

If we were to rule Al-Mas'oudi's narration for the reasons we mentioned above, we are left with the three remaining narrations. These narrations share the commonality of relying on eyewitnesses that were on the battlefield; however, they differ in the number of companions they report were with Imam Hussain (a). The discrepancy between the narrations of Abu

Mikhnif and Ammar Al-Duhani is about half, and that between Al-Duhani and Ibn Abdul-Rahman is about one third.

Nonetheless, we lean towards accepting all three narrations for the following reasons:

One, we find it very unlikely that these narrations would be based on lies in regards to the numbers provided, regardless of the narrator's emotional or ideological perspective of the revolution.

Two, these narrations don't describe the number of companions for one specific time and place. Rather, they each describe a different situation and context with regards to the number of men present with Imam Hussain (a).

Ammar Al-Duhani's narration, relating from Abu Ja'far (a), reflects the situation of Imam Hussain's (a) arrival in Karbala on the 2nd of Muharram. The other two narrations give context on the 10th of Muharram – 9 days later – which by that time there were definitely some changes in the number of men with the Imam (a). Some abandoned the companions of the Imam (a), while others joined the ranks, and some were sent by Imam Hussain (a) to deliver important messages to Basra and other cities.

The narration by Al-Duhani describes the total number of men that were with Imam Hussain (a) on that day – including Arabs, non-Arabs, Hashimites, non-Hashimites, and servants and aides that would not necessarily be considered fighters. It was natural for there to be a considerable number of such persons – servants and aides – with the Imam (a) and the families of the caravan. Again, we emphasize that the number presented by the narrator definitely is subject to error given the fact that the eyewitness estimated the total of companions by merely the use of his naked eye.

The narration by Al-Husseyn ibn Abdul-Rahman reflects the situation of the 10th of Muharram before the outbreak of battle. It described the number of fighters – Hashimites, Arabs and non-Arabs alike. The group of servants however was not included in this illustration to be reflected in the narration. If they were the narration would have said the number to be well over one hundred, instead of stating that it was near a hundred as it does. This allows us to infer that the narration reflects the position of Imam Hussain's (a) camp before he mobilized the formations of his forces. In addition, it seems that some of the men might have been too far for the eyewitness of the narration to see and count them. Remember, the narration depends on the vision of the eyewitness without access to any proper tools of statistics. Moreover, there were young Hashimites that were also martyred in the battle of Karbala that were not taken into account by the narrator.

Abu Mikhnif's narration, along with other narrations that agree with it, reflect the situation after Imam Hussain (a) mobilized his forces. By our assessment, the narration describes the number of non-Hashimite Arab fighters amongst the supporters of Imam Hussain (a). Thus, the number does not include the Hashimites, the non-Arabs, or the servants.

The text of Al-Mas'oudi supports this opinion. His narration says, "… And forty-some fought alongside him from his companions – of the preceding totals – from the rest of the Arabs."[19] Before this he said regarding the number of those killed with Imam Hussain (a): "And the total of those killed with Hussain on the day of Ashura in Karbala was eighty-seven, amongst them was his son Ali ibn Hussain Al-Akbar."[20] Thus, it must be that this total was not encompassing the non-Arabs and the servants and aides. He clearly refers to the supporters of the Arabs, and we know for certain that there was a significant number of non-Arabs that were supporters and companions of Imam Hussain (a) present. They were not included in the tallies of martyrs due to the racist mentality that was ever so prevalent with people at the time. Because of their racism they simply ignored their presence and did not consider the non-Arabs.[21] Moreover, if we take out the number of Hashimites from the total mentioned by Al-Mas'oudi it would come out to be about the same count as Abu Mikhnif, who did not include the Hashimites or non-Arabs. This of course includes the consideration for the margin of error that comes with approximation by the naked eye, even if the margin of error is very slim for the following two reasons.

Firstly, the narrator is Al-Dhahhak ibn Abdullah Al-Mashriqi – one of the companions of Imam Hussain (a) – and is in a prime position to deliver the most accurate estimate.

Secondly, this estimate reflects the situation in the context of Imam Hussain's (a) forces standing in formation, which allows for a more accurate estimate of those present. The number that this narration encompasses is seventy-two cavalry and infantry, and the number that this study ends with is approximately one hundred. If we are to subtract twenty men – representing ten servants of Imam Hussain (a), two servants of Imam Ali (a), and eight others – we are left with seventy-eight non-Hashimite Arab companions. This is before Al-Hur ibn Yazid Al-Riyahi abandoned the camp of Yazid and joined the camp of Imam Hussain (a). Based on this, the margin of error in our conclusion or in the narration by Abu Mikhnif is very nominal. And such a discrepancy is ordinary given such circumstances.

* * *

There still remains a few issues with regards to the number of Imam Hussain's (a) companions.

One of the issues comes to the forefront by a narration related by Al-Sayyid ibn Tawous in his book Al-Luhouf fi Qatl Al-Tufouf. He states,

> … *Hussain and his companions stayed up on that night (the 10th night of Muharram), their camp buzzing like a beehive, with some prostrating, bowing, rising and*

kneeling in prayer. In that night, thirty-two men from the camp of Umar ibn Saad switched over to their camp.[22]

We stand skeptical before this narration.

First, because a narration like this should have grabbed the attention of other narrators. This kind of event is unique and definitely relevant to this discourse on the number of supporters with Imam Hussain (a). Therefore, others would have naturally narrated it as well had it truly occurred. But the fact that other direct narrators did not mention this pushes us to doubt the authenticity of this narration.

Secondly, this number – thirty-two – is a big number in perspective of the small group of supporters Imam Hussain (a) had. Thus, it would only reasonably follow that they would have had a felt impact on the size and force of Imam Hussain's (a) army the morning of Ashura. This is especially given that they had supposedly joined just the night before, even though we haven't witnessed any kind of observation of such an impact from the narrations.

Because of this, we lean towards this number being unreliable in the circle of our study of the supporters of Imam Hussain (a). It is more likely that the men who supposedly joined the camp of Imam Hussain (a), didn't really join him, but instead left the camp of Yazid and decided not to participate in the battle. This would have been due to an internal struggle of conscience realizing the heinous crimes that Yazid's camp was intent on committing, and the self-interest of staying alive and not being prey to such a criminal body. So, they left one camp but didn't join the other.

It seems that much of this did occur in reality. Take the example of Masrouq ibn Wael Al-Hadrami, who had the ambition to strike the head of Imam Hussain (a) for a hefty reward from Ibn Ziyad… but he abandoned the battle and left the army when he saw what happened to Ibn Houza when Imam Hussain (a) prayed against him. Masrouq said, "I saw something from this household that turned me away from ever wanting to fight them."[23]

Perhaps those men were the same petty men that Al-Husseyn ibn Abdel-Rahman mentioned in his narration to be standing on the hilltop crying and saying, "God bring down your victory!"

* * *

Another issue that is related to the number of Imam Hussain's (a) supporters is the gruesome picture of the heads placed on spears by the soldiers of Yazid.

The narrations agree on what seems to be an almost firm number of heads that were severed at the end of the battle. Those heads were placed on spears and sent to Kufa and then Syria thereafter. The number narrated is between seventy and seventy-five.

Abu Mikhnif illustrates what took place after Imam Hussain's (a) head was severed. He relays the narration from Qurra ibn Qays Al-Tamimi, an eyewitness from the Umayyad army. "… The remaining heads were severed and seventy-two heads were taken…"[24]

Al-Daynouri said, "The heads were held at the tips of the spears… there were seventy-two."[25]

Shaykh Al-Mufid said, "… On the day of Ashura, Umar ibn Saad ordered that the head of Hussain (a) be taken by Khawla ibn Yazid Al-Asbahi and Hameed ibn Muslim to Ubaydallah ibn Ziyad. He then ordered for the rest of the heads of the Imam's (a) companions and family members be severed – they were seventy-two heads."[26]

Al-Majlisi narrates in Bihar Al-Anwar, from Muhammad ibn Abi Talib Al-Mousawi, "… The heads of the companions and family members of Imam Hussain (a) were seventy-eight."[27]

The narrations also provide numbers with context to the specific distribution of the severed heads to the tribes.

Abu Mikhnif narrates, "… The Kindah tribe, amongst them Qays ibn Al-Ash'ath, carried thirteen severed heads; the Hawazan tribe, amongst them Shimr ibn Thil-Jawshan, carried twenty heads; the Banu Asad tribe carried six heads; the Muthhij tribe carried seven, and the rest of the army carried another seven. They were seventy heads in total."[28] Note that

Abu Mikhnif mentions in his previous narration that "seventy-two heads were taken..."

Al-Daynouri narrates, "...The heads were held at the tips of the spears... there were seventy-two. The Hawazan tribe came with twenty-two; the Tamim tribe, with Al-Husseyn ibn Nameer, held seventeen; the Kindah tribe, with Qays ibn Al-Ash'ath, held thirteen heads; the Banu Asad tribe, with Hilal ibn Al-A'war, held six; the Azd tribe, with 'Ayhama ibn Zuheir, held five heads; and the Thaqif tribe, with Al-Waleed ibn Amr, held twelve heads."[29]

Though Al-Daynouri says the total number of heads were seventy-two, if we add up the mentioned numbers by each tribe the total comes out to be seventy-five.

Muhammad ibn Abi Talib Al-Mousawi narrates, "... The Kindah tribe, with Qays ibn Al-Ash'ath, came with thirteen severed heads; the Hawazan tribe, with Shimr, held twelve heads; Banu Asad held six; the Muthhij tribe held seven, and the remainder of the people held thirteen severed heads."[30] The number of heads counted here is one the lower counts, accounting for only sixty-one in total.

It can be said that the total number of severed heads could indicate two things: the number of supporters in the camp of Imam Hussain (a) and/or the number of those who were martyred in the camp of the Imam (a).

If this were the case then it contradicts our theory on the number of companions with Imam Hussain (a), rather it contradicts all the prevalent narrations on this issue. It is established that the severed heads belonged to the Hashimites and non-Hashimites alike. That would mean that the non-Hashimite companions of the Imam (a) would have to be less than fifty men.

However, we don't see the number of severed heads on spears as a proof for this at all. The severing of the heads and propping them on spears from Karbala to Kufa and Kufa to Syria was an act of vengeance with political undertones, or a political move with undertones of vengeance. Such an act is subject to particular politics and policies, which we will discuss later on the book God willing.

Between all of the narrations mentioned on this specific subject, there are contradicting numbers of reported severed heads on spears: sixty-one, seventy, seventy-two, seventy-five, and seventy-eight. Abu Mikhnif by himself reports two different numbers at seventy-two and seventy, while Al-Daynouri does the same at seventy-two and seventy-five. This is in addition to the differences between the narrations on the number of severed heads held by each tribe.

These discrepancies evidence that this issue, as seen in these narrations, is not as simple as it may seem. The situations in themselves are very complicated. Such complications are linked to the relationships of the tribes with those killed from one aspect and are connected to the political status of the tribe from another. Nonetheless we will study this issue further in what is to come.

* * *

Were all of the companions of Imam Hussain (a) killed or did some survive?

Abu Mikhnif narrates from Muhammad ibn Muslim who was an eyewitness from the Umayyad army,

> … *Seventy-two men were killed from the supporters of Hussain… and eighty-eight were killed from the supporters of Umar ibn Saad, other than the wounded…*[31]

This narration describes the number of non-Hashimite martyrs. Without a doubt, this narration is false with regards to the number of dead in the Umayyad army. The lowest of estimates provided in the vast majority of narrations give a much higher number than the one mentioned here.

Al-Mas'oudi said, "And the total of those killed with Hussain on the day of Ashura in Karbala was eighty-seven, amongst them was his son Ali ibn Hussain Al-Akbar."[32] This narrations encompasses both Hashimites and non-Hashimites with the fact that the narrator mentions Ali ibn Hussain (a).

In another narration by Hisham ibn Al-Waleed Al-Kalbi and Abu Mikhnif on Yazid ibn Muawiya's welcoming of Ubaydallah ibn Ziyad's messenger, who was sent as a messenger to end the threat of Hussain's (a) revolution, it says:

... Zehr ibn Qays came before Yazid ibn Muawiya. Yazid told him, 'What caused you to come and what news do you bear?' He answered, 'I give glad tidings, o' prince of the believers, of God's victory and support. We intercepted Hussain ibn Ali and eighteen of his family members, along with sixty of his followers. We surrounded them from every angle until we met them with their end...[33]

To accept any one of these narrations would mean that not all of Imam Hussain's (a) companions were killed, instead many of them should have escaped death. But we can't accept such a conclusion, just as we can't accept the narrations themselves even if we were to agree with their findings. We lean towards rejecting these narrations because in their context the numbers they provide should have been based on solid statistics. The total number of those killed should be an unruffled topic. There was no danger in gathering the data because their enemies couldn't attack them or fight back since they were already dead. They had complete control over the battlefield. The battle was over. If this was the case, they could have easily counted them one by one and gathered this very basic statistic, especially since the total with all the minor discrepancies was so small in number.

Statistics would mandate for the narrators to be in agreement in relaying the total number of deaths, considering the fact that they would be eyewitnesses. Given that the narrators have differed considerably, their precision is thrown into question. Furthermore, it goes to say that they most probably excluded the non-Arabs in the totals they provided. Even if we were to give this narrations the benefit of the doubt we would need to assume that some of the martyrs were buried before the end of the battle. Thus, due to their burials they were not counted in the totals mentioned in these narrations. Admittedly, we don't have any proof or evidence to support such a premise.

Similarly, we can't accept such a conclusion. All of the sources of history, without exception, say that Imam Hussain (a) was the last one standing the battlefield from his camp. After all his companions were martyred and then all the fighters from his family were martyred he stood alone on the sands of Karbala. He fought until the very end. He was martyred. Alone.

None of the primary or secondary sources mention that any of his companions ever abandoned him. Nor do any of the sources mention that any of the males in the camp survived except the following individuals below:

The Hashimites:

1) Imam Ali ibn Hussain ibn Ali ibn Abi Talib, Zayn Al-Abideen (a)

2) Hassan ibn Hassan ibn Ali ibn Abi Talib

3) Umar ibn Hassan ibn Ali ibn Abi Talib[34]

The non-Hashimites:

1) Al-Dhahhak ibn Abdullah Al-Mashriqi. He joined the camp of the Imam (a) with the condition that he would be given leave when he saw that his fighting would no longer be of any benefit to defending the Imam (a).[35]

2) 'Aqaba ibn Sam'aan, the servant of Rabab – Imam Hussain's (a) wife. He said to Umar ibn Saad when he was just about to be killed, "I am [just] a slave." He was let go.[36]

3) Al-Muraqqa' ibn Thumama Al-Asadi. He took out his arrows, positioned himself with knees to the ground and fought the enemies. He fought until he was surrounded. A group of his fellow tribesman came to him from the other camp and took him under their protection.[37]

These are the only males that have been established as having been saved from the massacre. If any of the men had deserted Hussain (a) during or before the battle, or had survived thereafter, his name would have been remembered.

The consensus of the narrations we have mentioned, in addition to the lack of consistency in the narrations themselves, push us not to rely on them and to disregard them as proper proofs for the total number of companions or the true number of martrys with Imam Hussain (a).

The following narration by Ammar Al-Duhani is largely truthful in this regard: "All of the companions of Hussain were killed, amongst them were a little over ten members of his family."[38]

* * *

What role did the Hashimites play in the fighting force of Imam Hussain's (a) army on the 10th of Muharram?

Were the Hashimites on the morning of Ashura present as part of the fighting force that Imam Hussain (a) mobilized, whereby he assigned Zuhair ibn Al-Qayn the right flank, Habibi ibn Mudaher the left flank, and his brother Al-Abbas (a) as the flag-bearer? Or were the Hashimites outside of this fighting force?

We view that the first suggestion is true – they were part and parcel of the initiation fighting force and formation mobilized by the Imam (a). It would be absurd to consider the idea that the Hashimites, Imam Hussain's (a) family, would sit comfortably in their tents as their non-Hashimite companions were in formation to fight in battle. It is true that the non-Hashimites were the first to commence, fight, and be martyred; however, the Hashimites were all in formation within the mobilized force. They all stood together in the same place ready for battle.

On this issue, Al-Khawarizmi narrates,

> *... Hussain mobilized his companions... he assigned the right flank to Zuhair ibn Al-Qayn, the left flank to Habib ibn Mudaher, the flag to his brother Al-Abbas ibn Ali (a), and based himself and his family members at the heart of the formation.*[39]

The station of the flag-bearer, in the formation, was at the center – the heart. Thus, when a narration mentions that the flag was in the hands of Abbas ibn Ali (a) it also indicates that the Hashimites were at the center with Imam Hussain (a).[40] This is with the exception of the young boys that were not old enough to fight. Some of them were still martyred. A few of the young boys rushed into the battlefield to protect Imam Hussain (a) in his final moments when no one else was left to defend him. They were killed.

* * *

It was possible for the number of supporters to Imam Hussain (a) to be considerably greater than they were. Such an increase would not have changed the result of the battle itself, but it would have made the battle longer and more challenging to the Umayyad forces. The combination of increased forces to the revolution and some assisting political mechanisms, if actualized, could have changed the outcome of the battle. This was all possible if not for some obstacles.

A few days before the battle, Habib ibn Mudaher asked Imam Hussain (a) if he could call on some of his tribesmen from Banu Asad that were near Karbala to come to their aid. The Imam (a) gave him leave to do so. Habib's tribesmen accepted his request to support Imam Hussain (a) and ninety ready fighters came forth. Umar ibn Saad became aware of this and quickly assembled four hundred cavalry.

> *The tribesmen from Banu Asad mobilized in the dark of the night with Habib making their way to the camp of Hussain. Ibn Saad's cavalry intercepted them at the shores of the Furat River. There was only a short distance between them and the camp of Hussain. The two groups disputed and sparred. Then Habib shouted at Al-Arzaq ibn Al-Harth, 'What business do you have with us? Leave us now! I'm warning you, let us be and bother someone else.' Al-Arzaq refused. Banu Asad knew that they could not defeat Ibn Saad's cavalry. Outnumbered, they retreated to their neighborhood in defeat. They took cover in the dark of the night fearing that Ibn Saad would catch them. Habib returned to Hussain and informed him of what took place.[41]*

The regime feared that if people heard what was taking place in Karbala it would only increase and strengthen Imam Hussain's (a) camp. Therefore, it rushed to crush the movement and defeat Imam Hussain's (a) small band of family and companions. The regime refused to entertain any form of negotiation or political engagement, even reprimanding Umar ibn Saad for simply speaking to Imam Hussain (a). The regime ordered the Umayyad army to cut off the water supply from Hussain's (a) camp not simply to torture them physically. They wanted to suppress any fighting power Imam Hussain (a) and his small force had, weaken their horses, and create a heart wrenching for the camp seeing their own women and children dying of thirst.

Habib ibn Mudaher's attempt to rally supporters from Banu Asad also alerted the leadership of the Umayyad army to Imam Hussain's (a) supporters that were coming from near the Furat River. This led the Umayyads to further bolster their forces guarding the river and ensure no water or supporter will reach the camp of Imam Hussain (a).[42]

Corroborating this is a passing note in a narration for Al-Tabari relating the words of one of the soldiers in the Umayyad army. It illustrates one of the tragic heart wrenching scenes of the 10th of Muharram.

> *He who saw Hussain in his camp told me that when Hussain's supporters were all killed, Hussain rode his horse toward the Furat. A man named Ibn Darim from the Banu Abaan tribe called out, 'Beware! Don't let him reach the water! Don't let his Shia reach him!'[43]*

That statement, "Don't let his Shia reach him…" mentioned as a reason to prevent Hussain (a) from the water shows that the Umayyad leadership was well aware of the reinforcements coming to Imam Hussain (a). The siege they created around the river was not simply to prevent Hussain's (a) camp from water, but to prevent his other supporters from joining the fight. They were ready to join and come to his aid. Perhaps some of them were the same tribesmen from Banu Asad that were unable to reach him earlier with Habib ibn Mudaher.

WHO WERE THEY?

In this chapter we will discuss the names of the martyrs of Karbala – names that were forever etched in history by their noble sacrifice. We strive to unravel as much about them as possible, from their personalities and character to their tribes and social environment. This is with the disclaimer that the number may not be exact. There could be a portion of names that we have not come to due to the negligence of historians and narrators. In addition, some persons may be repeated more than once because they were mentioned in the narrations by alternative names or nicknames, without us having the tools to differentiate for sure between each name, title, or nickname. Nonetheless, we are confident that the margin of error in this regard is only nominal.

The typographical errors found in the names, nicknames, and lineages during this portion of study to showcase the true names and profiles of the martyrs has been the most vexing of all. Thus, as a cautionary measure for precision we have created two groups. The first includes the names of the martyrs, may

God be pleased with them. The second includes the names of the men who are presumably amongst the martyrs of Karbala. In the first group we have established the names of the martyrs that have been mentioned in *Ziyaret Al-Nahiya Al-Muqaddasa*, because it is the oldest document that encompasses what is considered to be all of the martyrs. We are using this simply as a historical record for reference, because its religious significance is not completely established as we have mentioned previously. In the same token, we have established names to be included this first group that were not mentioned in the Ziyara. However, they were cited in other primary sources such as *Rijal Al-Shaykh Al-Tousi* or *Al-Tabari*, or were named independently in two secondary sources, or at least that two secondary sources listed the name as a martyr. We gave close care to ensure that one of the two sources in this regards would be a primary source. The second group includes names that are only mentioned by some of the later sources such as *Ziyaret Al-Rajabiya, Kitab ibn Shahr Ashoub, Mutheer Al-Ahzan*, or *Al-Luhouf* and its likes.

You will find that the information available is very little. And even the little that exists out there is not easily accessible due to the negligence of historians from one aspect and the typographical errors from another. Such errors have swapped names and entire lineages from one person to another. Still, this little information will be of great value if we are able to categorize it and study its semantics and implications properly. We will see that it unveils for us new dimensions to this revolution that we would never have come to before without studying the lives of these champions, these heroes.

The names displayed below are arranged in alphabetical order[1], with mention to the individual's social groups, tribes, geography, and racial background.

THE MARTYRS OF KARBALA

1. ASLEM AL-TURKI, THE SERVANT OF HUSSAIN (A)

Al-Tabari mentions him by the name *Sulayman*.[1] He is also mentioned by this name in the Ziyara[2] and by Sayyid Al-Ameen. Shaykh Al-Tousi mentions him in Al-Rijal stating, "Sulaym, the servant of Hussain (a), fought alongside him."[3] We find it more likely that this man that was martyred in Karbala was named Aslem and not Sulayman or Sulaym. Shaykh Al-Tousi mentioned him in Al-Rijal but did not say that he was martyred. In A'yan Al-Shia, Sayyid Al-Ameen mentions him in his index and, in describing the saga, states "… and then came forth a young Turkish servant for Hussain (a) named Aslem…"[4] Al-Sayyid Al-Ustath[5] also mentions this in his book Mu'jam Rijal Al-Hadeeth.[6] Certainly this must be what was intended by those who narrated, "… and then came forth a young Turkish servant for Hussain (a)…"[7] but did not mention his name.

Sulayman was also a servant of Imam Hussain (a). In fact, he was his messenger to the people of Basra. One of the chieftains of Basra, Al-Munthir Ibn Al-Jaroud Al-'Abdi, reported him Ubaydallah ibn Ziyad – Yazid's governor of Basra at the time. Ibn Ziyad had Sulayman executed. Sulayman was also known by his *kunya* (title or agnomen) who was also known as Aba Ruzayn.[8]

The sources say that Aslem was a reciter of the Holy Quran, knowledgeable in the Arabic language, and a writer.

He was a servant, and nothing else is known about him.

2. ANAS IBN AL-HARITH AL-KAHILI

Shaykh Al-Tousi mentions him in Al-Rijal as one of the companions of the Messenger of God (s) noting that he was killed with Imam Hussain (a). At the same time he has been mentioned as one of the companions of the Imam Hussain (a) without specifically saying he was killed with him.[9] Sayyid Al-Khoei also mentions him,[10] which we believe is the same as *Anas ibn Kahil Al-Asadi* that was mentioned in Al-Ziyara and Al-Rajabiya. Though Sayyid Al-Khoei considered this name as a separate one,[11] they are most probably the same person since *Al-Kahili* is *Asadi*, meaning belonging to the Asad tribe, and *Ibn Kahil* is an indicator of lineage to that same tribe.

Ibn Shar Ashoub and Al-Khawarizmi both address him incorrectly as, "Malik ibn Anas Al-Kahili."[12] Al-Bihar also incorrectly writes his name as "Malik ibn Anas Al-Maliki," which was later corrected relating from Ibn Nama Al-Hilli.[13]

Known as Al-Kahili, he belonged to the Kahil clan from the tribe of Asad ibn Khuzayma of the 'Adnan bloodline. They were Arabs of the north.

Anas was a man of old age. Given his tenure and position as a companion of the Holy Prophet (s), he was widely respected and enjoyed reputable social status. It seems that he was from Kufa, as Muhammad ibn Saad mentions the homes of the Kahil clan were located in Kufa.[14]

3. ANEES IBN MA'QIL AL-ASBAHI

Anees is mentioned by Shar Ashoub,[15] Al-Khawarizmi,[16] and Sayyid Al-Ameen. Known as Al-Asbahi, he belong to the Asabih clan from the tribes of Qahtan – located in Yemen and most Arabs of the south. No other details about his background are reported.

4. UM WAHAB BINT ABED

Um Wahab was from the lineage of Al-Nimr ibn Qasit. She was the wife of Abdullah ibn Umayr Al-Kalbi who was from the Bani Uleem tribe. He told his wife, Um Wahab, that he was intent on joining the caravan of Imam Hussain (a). "You've made the right decision. May God employ you on what is right and guide your path. Go forth and take me with you," she answered. They left in the night until they reached Imam Hussain (a).

When her husband went into the battlefield he killed two of Umar ibn Saad's soldiers. At that point, "Um Wahab grabbed a rod and rushed towards her husband saying to him, 'May my mother and father be sacrificed for you, fight in protection of the pure progeny of Muhammad!' He came to her and urged her to go back to the camp. She pulled on his clothes and said, 'I will not leave you until I die by your side.' Imam Hussain (a) then called her, 'May God reward your family the best of rewards. Come back to the women and be with them. God bless you. Women are not obliged to fight.' Upon that she went back to the women... After her husband was martyred she went back into the battlefield and sat herself next to his body. Wiping the sand from his face she said, 'Glad tidings, you earned your place in heaven.' Shimr ibn Thil-Jawshan told a young soldier by the name of Rustom, 'Go and strike her on the head with a pole.' He went forth, struck her on the head and killed her in her place."[17]

5. BURAYR IBN KHUDAYR AL-HAMADANI

Burayr is mentioned by Al-Tabari,[18] Ibn Shahr Ashoub,[19] and Al-Majlisi in Bahr Al-Anwar misspelling his name as "Budayr ibn Hufayr"[20]. Burayr is also mentioned in Al-Rajabiya. Sayyid Al-Khoei also mentions Burayr but as "Burayr ibn Al-Husseyn" referencing Al-Rajabiya.[21] It seems that the copy he referenced at the time also had a typographical error, writing "Husseyn" instead of "Khudayr."

Burayr had tried to dissuade Umar ibn Saad from his allegiance to the Umayyad regime. The sources say that he was "the Master of Reciters," a scholar, a monk, a reciter of the Quran, and a teacher of the Quran in the university of Kufa. Amongst the Hamadanis he had the highest of respect, honor and nobility. He was also widely known and respected in Kufan society.[22]

As a Hamadani, he was of the Kahlan people who were southern Arabs from Yemen. Burayr's hometown was Kufa.

6. BUSHAYR IBN AMR AL-HADRAMI

Al-Tabari says that he was one of the last two companions that were killed before the Hashimites took to the frontlines of the battlefield. The other companion was Suwayd ibn Amr ibn Abu Al-Moutaa'.[23] He is also mentioned in Al-Rajabiya and in Al-Ziyara mistakenly as "Bishr ibn Umar Al-Hadrami."[24] Sayyid Al-Ameen mentions him as "Bishr ibn Abdullah Al-Hadrami."

Sayyid Al-Khoei mentions both possibilities of Bishr and Bushayr.[25] Sayyid ibn Tawous mentions "Muhammad ibn Bushayr Al-Hadrami," who we are certain is the same individual, as the Ibn Tawous tells the same story of this individual's son.[26] This is the same story that is narrated in Al-Ziyara, which mentions the name Bishr or Bushayr, depending on the referenced manuscript.

Al-Hadrami refers to being form the Hadhramowt, a tribe from the Qahtan bloodline. From this tribe the name of the Hadhramowt Province was coined. It could also refer to the clan of Al-Hadrami, an off-shoot of the tribe of Thabi from the Yafi' bloodline in Yemen. Bushayr was also counted amongst the Kindah tribe, which is also a tribe from Yemen. He was a southern Arab belonging to Yemen.

The information found in the sources is limited to this.

7. JABIR IBN AL-HARITH AL-SALMANI

This is the way his name appears in Al-Tabari.[27] Shaykh Al-Tousi refers to him as "Junada ibn Al-Harath Al-Salmani"[28] with Sayyid Al-Ameen doing the same. Sayyid Al-Khoei referred to him as Junada as well relying on Shaykh Al-Tousi's reference.[29] At the same time he makes note of a "Hayyan ibn Al-Harith Al-Salmani Al-Azdi" as a separate person.[30]

In one version of Al-Ziyara he is mentioned as "Habbab ibn Al-Harith Al-Salmani Al-Azdi"[31] and in another version as "Hayyan." In Bihar's version of Al-Rajabiya he is mentioned as "Hayyan ibn Al-Harith" and in the version found in Al-Iqbal it is "Hassaan ibn Al-Harith." Ibn Shahr Ashoub refers to him as "Habbab ibn Al-Harith," mentioning him as one of the martyrs in the first offensive during the battle of Karbala.[32]

He was one the known Shia personalities in Kufa. He joined the movement of Muslim ibn 'Aqeel in Kufa. After the revolution's failure in Kufa, he made his way to Imam Hussain (a) with a group of others. They met the Imam (a) not much before his arrival in Karbala. Al-Hur ibn Yazid Al-Riyahi tried to stop them from joining Imam Hussain (a), but he was unsuccessful.

Ibn Al-Harith was Salmani, from the bloodline of Murad and before him Muthhij. He was a southern Arab from Yemen.

The information found in the sources is limited to this.

8. JABALA IBN ALI AL-SHAYBANI

He is mentioned in Al-Ziyara[33] and is also mentioned by Ibn Shahr Ashoub as one of the companions that was martyred in the first offensive.[34] He is likely to be the same individual referred to as "Jabala ibn Abdullah" mentioned in Al-Rajabiya. Sayyid Al-Khoei mentions both names in his book.[35] Jabala participated in the movement of Muslim ibn 'Aqeel in Kufa. He was from the Shayban tribe which belongs to the bloodline of 'Adnan. Jabala was a northern Arab.

9. JUNADA IBN AL-HARITH AL-ANSARI

He is mentioned in Ibn Shar Ashoub's book[36] as well as by Al-Khawarizmi as "Junada ibn Al-Harath."[37] Bihar Al-Anwar also takes note of Junada.[38] He is known as being from the people of Ansar, and is a southern Arab from Yemen.

The information found in the sources is limited to this.

10. JUNDUB IBN HUJAYR AL-KHAWLANI

Shaykh Al-Tousi mentions Jundub without giving saying that he was martyred,[39] and was also mentioned in Al-Ziyara as "Jundub ibn Hajar Al-Khawlani"[40]. He is also mentioned in Al-Rajabiya as "Jundub ibn Hujayr" and is referenced thusly by Sayyid Al-Khoei[41], as well as by Sayyid Al-Ameen. As a Khawlani he is associated with the Kahlan tribe and is from the bloodline Qahtan. Jundub is from a southern Arab from Yemen.

The information found in the sources is limited to this.

11. JOHN THE SERVANT OF ABATHAR AL-GHAFARI

John is mentioned in Al-Rajabiya. He is also mentioned in Bihar Al-Anwar and in Al-Ziyara by the name "John ibn Hawi the Servant of Abathar Al-Ghafari"[42]. Shaykh Al-Tousi discusses him without particularly saying that he was martyred.[43] Furthermore, John is mentioned by Al-Khawarizmi,[44] while is referred to as "Hawi" by Al-Tabari.[45] Ibn Shahr Ashoub states his name as "Juwayn Abi Malik the Servant of Abathar Al-Ghafari."[46] John was a servant of dark complexion and an elderly man.

The information found in the sources is limited to this.

12. JUWAYN IBN MALIK AL-DHABA'I

Shaykh Al-Tousi mentions Juwayn amongst the companions of Imam Hussain (a) but does not specifically say that he was martyred.[47] He is mentioned in Al-Ziyara along with the names of the other martyrs. At times he is referred to with this name and other times as "Hawi ibn Malik Al-Dhaba'i. Some have mixed between him and John the Servant of Abathar. Furthermore, Juwayn is mentioned in Al-Rajabiya but as "Juwayr ibn Malik," which we expect is a typographical error just like other variations such as "Hawi" and "Jubar." Juwayn was one of the soldiers of Umar ibn Saad but deserted the Umayyad camp and joined the camp of Imam Hussain (a). He was killed in the first offensive of the battle. His name Al-Dhaba'i is a reference to his lineage from Dhaba' ibn Wabara who is from the bloodline of Qahtan. Juwayn is a southern Arab from Yemen.

Nothing is known of him.

13. HABIB IBN MUDAHER AL-ASADI

All of the sources have mentioned Habib. He is one the companions of Imam Ali ibn Abi Talib (a). He was selected as one of Imam Ali's (a) most trusted legionnaires. Imam Hussain (a) designated him as the leader of the left flank of his battalion during the mobilization of his forces for the battle of Karbala. It has been discussed previously that Habib attempted to rally supporters from his tribe, Banu Asad. The Umayyad forces prevented the group of fighters from getting to the camp of Hussain (a). Moreover, Habib was one of the Kufan chieftains that wrote to Imam Hussain (a) to come to Kufa.[48] He was honored by Imam Hussain (a). "When Habib ibn Mudaher was killed it devastated Hussain. He said, 'To my companions and myself, the deepest condolences.'"[49]

Habib was a prominent figure in Kufan society. He belonged to the Asad tribe and was from the bloodline of 'Adnan. Habib was a northern Arab.

14. AL-HAJJAJ IBN ZAYD AL-SAADI

Al-Hajjaj's name is stated in Al-Ziyara.[50] Sayyid Al-Ameen refers to him as "Al-Hajjaj ibn Badr Al-Saadi" and is cited as "Hajjaj ibn Yazid" in Al-Rajabiya. Sayyid Al-Khoei referred to him as "Al-Hajjaj ibn Yazid" stating that this is what he was cited as in Al-Ziyara.[51] However, the newer edition of Al-Bihar does not agree with the older edition in this regard.

Al-Hajjaj carried a letter form Mas'oud ibn Amr Al-Azadi to Imam Hussain (a) as a response to Imam Hussain's letter to Mas'oud and the rest of the chieftains of Kufan on the matter of their invitation to the Imam (a).

Al-Hajjaj is a Basri from the clan of Ban Saad, who belong to the Tamim tribe, from the bloodline of 'Adnan. Al-Hajjaj was a northern Arab.

The information found in the sources is limited to this.

15. AL-HAJJAJ IBN MASROUQ AL-JU'FI

He is mentioned in Al-Tabari,[52] in Al-Ziyara and in Bihar Al-Anwar.[53] He is also discussed by Al-Khawarizmi.[54] Al-Rajabiya mentions him as well. Ibn Shahr Ashoub states his name,[55] but is referred to as "Al-Hajjaj ibn Marzouq" by Shaykh Al-Tousi.[56] This is the name that Sayyid Al-Khoei uses in addressing Al-Hajjaj in Mu'jam Al-Rijal.[57] He also mentions Al-Hajjaj ibn Masrouq Al-Ju'fi under an independent name.[58] It seems that combining the two would be reasonable.

Al-Hajjaj left Kufa for Mecca and joined Imam Hussain (a) in Mecca to embark on his journey. Imam Hussain (a) ordered him perform the call to prayer for Salat Al-Thuhr (the Noon Prayer) at the time they were stopped by Al-Hur ibn Yazid. It is also narrated in some sources that he was Imam Hussain's (a) designated *Mu'athin* (Caller to Prayer). Al-Hajjaj was a Kufi. He belonged to the tribe of Ju'fi ibn Saad, which was from the lineage of Muthhij and the bloodline of Qahtan. Al-Hajjaj was a southern Arab originally from Yemen.

16. AL-HUR IBN YAZID AL-RIYAHI AL-YARBOU'I AL-TAMIMI

He is mentioned by all of the sources on this subject. Al-Hur is mentioned several times in Al-Rajabiya, both in the beginning and towards its end. He was regarded as one of the prominent personalities of Kufa. In addition, Al-Hur was one of the commanders of the Umayyad army in Karbala. In his battalion alone, he led one quarter of the Hamadan and Tamim tribesman of the Umayyad army.[59] With one thousand cavalry, Al-Hur met Imam Hussain (a) at the Thi-Husum. He was directed by Ubaydallah ibn Ziyad to counter Hussain's (a) movement.[60]

Al-Hur repented before the outbreak of battle and joined the camp of Imam Hussain (a). He fought and died for him.[61] Some sources on the saga of Karbala say that Al-Hur was empathetic to the movement from the point that he met the Imam (a).[62] We doubt that however. We imagine that this language was born out of the writers' being emotionally affected by Al-Hur's dramatic switch from being a general with the Umayyads to a martyr with Hussain (a). Some reputable secondary sources also say that the allegiance Al-Hur paid to the revolution in the last hour and him joining its ranks, had an impact on the positions taken by his son Ali ibn Al-Hur, his brother Mus'ab ibn Yazid, and his servant 'Urwa. This however has not been clearly established to us.[63]

Al-Riyahi belonged to the clan of Yarbou', from the tribe of Tamim and the bloodline of 'Adnan. Al-Hur was a Kufan, northern Arab. It seems more likely that he was a young man.

17. AL-HALLAS IBN AMR AL-RASIBI

Ibn Shahr Ashoub includes him in the number of companions martyred in the first offensive of the battle of Karbala.[64] Shaykh Al-Tousi refers to him as "Al-Hallash" and does not mention the details of his martyrdom.[65] In Al-Rajabiya he's mentioned as "Hallas ibn Amr," which is also used by Sayyid Al-Khoei.[66] In Mu'jam Al-Rijal, 6:189, he also mentions a "Hallas ibn Amr Al-Hijri," which it seems that he intended as a different person than the Hallas here. We consider the two to be the same person, and the title Al-Hijri would simply be a reference to his *hijra* – migration – from Yemen to Kufa. It does not contradict his lineage as Al-Rasibi.'

He was part of the Commander of the Faithful Imam Ali's (a) police force in the Kufa. It is also said that he and his brother, Al-Nu'man, were with Umar ibn Saad but then joined the camp of Imam Hussain (a). His brother will be mentioned later on in the list of martyrs. Al-Rasibi was a reference to the lineage of Rasib ibn Malik whom belonged to the Shanou'ah clan. They were from the tribe of Al-Azd, traced back to the Qahtan bloodline. Al-Hallas was a southern Arab, originally from Yemen, who settled in Kufa.

18. HANTHALA IBN AS'AD AL-SHABAMI

This is the manner in which Hanthala's name was mentioned in Al-Ziyara and in Al-Rajabiya. He is also referred to with "Saad" and "Al-Shaybani" in Bihar Al-Anwar.[67] He is mentioned by Al-Khawarizmi,[68] Al-Tabari,[69] Shaykh Al-Tousi,[70] and Sayyid Al-Ameen. Al-Shabami referred to the Shabam clan which was part of the Hamadan tribe. They belonged to the Qahtan bloodline. A southern Arab, Hanthala settled in Kufa but was originally from Yemen.

19. KHALID IBN AMR IBN KHALID AL-AZDI

Khalid is mentioned by Shahr Ashoub,[71] Al-Khawarizmi,[72] and Bihar Al-Anwar.[73] Al-Azdi refers to his tribe, Al-Azd. He was a young man. Khalid was a southern Arab from Yemen.

The information found in the sources is limited to this.

20. ZAHIR THE SERVANT OF AMR IBN AL-HAMQ AL-KHUZA'I

Shaykh Al-Tousi and Ibn Shar Ashoub list him among the companions that were killed in the first offensive of the battle of Karbala.[74] He is mentioned in Al-Rajabiya and in Al-Ziyara, particularly in the first of the two versions as "Zahid the Servant of Amr ibn Al-Hamq Al-Khuza'i."[75] In the second of the two, he is referred to as "Zahir." Sayyid Al-Khoei also mentions him in Mu'jam Al-Rijal.[76]

Citing to Al-Najashi in biographing Muhammad ibn Sinan, he says that this Zahir is the grandfather of Muhammad ibn Sinan. He was one of the companions of Imam Moussa Al-Kadhim (a) and Imam Ali Al-Rida (a). The narration, however, is very weak. Some of the sources also mistakenly refer to him as "Zahir ibn Amr Al-Kindi." He was one of the servants of the Kindah tribe. An elderly man, Zahir was from the respected personalities known in Kufa.

21. ZUHAYR IBN BISHR AL-KHATH'AMI

This is how his name was presented in this version of Al-Bihar,[77] and in another version as "Zuhayr ibn Saleem Al-Azdi." Ibn Shahr Ashoub mentions him as one of the martyrs in the first offensive of the battle.[78] We find it sensible that this Zuhayr and "Zuhayr ibn Saleem Al-Azdi," who is also mentioned by Ibn Shahr Ashoub, to be the same person. The same would be said about Al-Rajabiya's reference to "Zuhayr ibn Basheer." The title Al-Khath'ami is a reference lineage to Khath'am ibn Anmar ibn Arash – a tribe from the Qahtan bloodline. Zuhayr was a southern Arab from Yemen.

22. ZUHAYR IBN AL-QAYN AL-BUJALI

All of the sources mention this Zuhayr. In Al-Ziyara he was addressed with a special honorable way,[79] as well as being mentioned in Al-Rajabiya. He joined Imam Hussain (a) on the road from Mecca to Iraq after dreading to face him.[80] On the battlefield in Karbala he would confront the Umayyad army before the start of the battle.[81] Imam Hussain (a) assigned Zuhayr to lead the right flank of the companions' battalion.[82] He was a prominent figure in Kufan society and was seemingly of old age at the time. Al-Bujali refers to his lineage from the tribes of Anmar, Arash, and Kahlan, which are derived from the bloodline of Qahtan. Zuhayr was a southern Arab originally from Yemen.

23. ZAYD IBN MA'QAL AL-JU'FI

This is the manner in which he was mentioned in Al-Ziyara. In another version he is listed as "Badr ibn Ma'qal Al-Ju'fi," which is the name used by Sayyid Al-Khoei in Mu'jam Rijal Al-Hadith.[83] Shaykh Al-Tousi mentions him without speaking of his martyrdom. We believe that he is the same as "Munder ibn Al-Mufdhil Al-Ju'fi" who is mentioned in Al-Rajabiya. Al-Ju'fi was from the Muthhij tribe. He was a southern Arab from Yemen. The information provided in the sources is limited to this.

24. SALIM THE SERVANT OF BANU AL-MADANIYA AL-KALBI

A servant of Banu Al-Madaniya, Salim is mentioned in Al-Ziyara.[84] Banu Al-Madaniya is from the tribe of Kalb ibn Wabara who are from the bloodline of Qahtan. They are southern Arabs from Yemen. He was a servant, but the information found in the sources is limited to this.

25. SALIM THE SERVANT OF AMER IBN MUSLIM AL-'ABDI

He is mentioned in Al-Ziyara[85] and by Sayyid Al-Ameen. Al-'Abdi was from the tribe of Abdel-Qays, which belongs to the bloodline of 'Adnan. They were northern Arabs. Salim was a servant from Basra. The information found in the sources is limited to this.

26. SAAD IBN HANTHALA AL-TAMIMI

Saad is mentioned by both Shahr Ashoub[86] and Bihar Al-Anwar.[87] In Qamous Al-Rijal, Al-Tustari argues that this is the same person as Hanthala ibn As'ad Al-Shabami that we have listed and discussed above. We argue, however, that this Saad is indeed a different person than the Hanthala above. Ibn Shahr Ashoub mentions Saad from the *maqtal* of Muhammad ibn Abi Talib Al-Hashimi, the same is related by Al-Majlisi in Al-Bihar. Moreover, Shabami is a southern Arab while Tamimi here is a northern Arab. A discrepancy or typographical error in this case seems to be highly unlikely. Al-Tamimi was from the bloodline of 'Adnan. Saad was a northern Arab.

The information provided in the sources is limited to this.

27. SAAD IBN ABDULLAH THE SERVANT OF AMR IBN KHALID

Shaykh Al-Tousi[88] and Al-Tabari[89] mention Saad, but he is referred to as "Saeed" in Al-Ziyara.[90] It seems that he is the one mentioned in Al-Rajabiya in the line: "Peace be upon Amr ibn

Khalaf and Saeed, his servant…" Khalaf here would be a typographical error for Khalid.

Amr ibn Khalid Al-Asadi Al-Saydawi joined the camp of Imam Hussain (a) with his servant and some others. They were about to reach the Imam (a) when they were blockaded by Al-Hur ibn Yazid Al-Riyahi. Al-Hur tried to prevent them from joining Imam Hussain (a) but he was unable to deter them. Finally, regarding Saad – he was a servant and the information provided in the sources is limited to this.

28. SAEED IBN ABDULLAH AL-HANAFI

Saeed is mentioned by Al-Tabari,[91] Al-Khawarizmi,[92] Ibn Shahr Ashoub,[93] Al-Rajabiya, in Al-Ziyara by the name of "Saad,"[94] and Ibn Tawous.[95] Saeed was one of the messengers who delivered the letters of the Kufans to Imam Hussain (a).[96] He was one of the greatest of the revolutionaries with regards to spirit and morale. His title, Al-Hanafi, refers to the clan of Hanifa ibn Lujaym, which belonged to the tribe of Bakr ibn Wael. They were of the 'Adnan bloodline. Saeed was an Arab of the North.

29. SIWAR IBN MUN'IM IBN HABIS AL-HAMADANI AL-NUHAMI

Shaykh Al-Tousi and Ibn Shahr Ashoub include him as one of those killed in the first offenseive of the battle.[97] Ibn Shahr Ashoub refers to him as "Siwar ibn Abi Umayr Al-Nuhami"[98], while Al-Ziyara mentions him as "Siwar ibn Abi Humayr Al-Nuhami."[99] Sayyid Al-Khoei includes "Siwar ibn Abi Umayr" and "Siwar ibn Al-Mun'im" in his book.[100] He separated them as two individuals. We find it to be more apparent to consolidate the two as they are the same person and the discrepancy here is essentially due to a typographical error.

He was brought forth as a prisoner of war to Umar ibn Saad. The extent of his battle wounds caused him to pass away six months later. Al-Nuhami refers to the Nuham clan of the Hamadan tribe. They were from the Qahtan bloodline. Siwar was a southern Arab from Yemen.

30. SUWAYD IBN AMR IBN ABI AL-MOUTAA' AL-KHATH'AMI

Al-Tabari[101] and Shaykh Al-Tousi[102] discuss him. In Bihar Al-Anwar he is described as being "a noble man who prayed very much."[103] Ibn Shahr Ashoub referred to him, due to typographical error, as "Amr ibn Abi Al-Moutaa' Al-Ju'fi."[104] He was one of the last two companions to be martyred with Imam Hussain (a). He actually died after Imam Hussain (a) was killed. He was lying on the ground taking his last breaths, when he heard people shouting, "Hussain has been killed!" At that point "… he roused up and grabbed the knife that was still on him, his sword was taken. He fought the enemies with his knife for an hour, until he was finally killed… and he was the last martyr."[105] The title Al-Khath'ami is a reference lineage to Khath'am ibn Anmar ibn Arash – a tribe from the Qahtan bloodline. Suwayd was a southern Arab from Yemen.

31. SAYF IBN AL-HARITH IBN SURAYE' AL-JABIRI

He is mentioned by Al-Tabari[106] and Al-Khawarizmi.[107] He is also mentioned by Al-Ziyara as "Shubayb ibn Al-Harith"[108] and in Al-Rajabiya as "Sayf ibn Al-Harith." We will also discuss his cousin, Malik ibn Abd ibn Saree'. The title Al-Jabiri is a reference to the clan of Bani Jabir who are from the Hamadan tribe of Kahlan. They are southern Arabs from Yemen. In addition, it seems that he was a young man.

32. SAYF IBN MALIK AL-'ABDI

He is mentioned in Al-Ziyara as "Sayf ibn Malik"[109], likewise in Al-Rijal by Shaykh Al-Tousi.[110] Ibn Shahr Ashoub discusses him as one of the martyred companions killed in the first offenseive of the battle, but as "Sayf ibn Malik Al-Numayri."[111] Al-Rajabiya refers to him as "Sufyan ibn Malik." Sayf was amongst the group of men that would meet at the house of Maria bint Munqith Al-'Abdiya in Basra. Maria's home was a gathering place for the Shia.[112] Al-'Abdi refers to being of the lineage of Abdel-Qays who was from the bloodline of 'Adnan. He was a northern Arab.

33. HABIB IBN ABDULLAH AL-NAHSHALI

Habib is mentioned by Shaykh Al-Tousi,[113] Al-Ziyara,[114] and Al-Rajabiya. He is perhaps the same individual as Abu Amr Al-Nahshali who is considered to be a separate person by Ibn Nama Al-Hilli in Mutheer Al-Ahzan. Al-Nahshali refers to being from the clan of Nahshal ibn Darim, who belonged to the tribe of Tamim. They are of the bloodline of 'Adnan. Habib was a northern Arab.

34. SHAWTHAB THE SERVANT OF SHAKIR IBN AB- DULLAH AL-HAMADANI AL-SHAKIRI

Shawthab is mentioned by Al-Tabari,[115] Shaykh Al-Tousi,[116] Al-Khawarizmi,[117] Al-Ziyara,[118] and Al-Rajabiya. Al-Rajabiya, however, refers to him as "Suwayd the Servant of Shakir." He was counted as one of the true men amongst the Shia, a prominent figure in his own right. Shawthab was one of the greatest of the revolutionaries in his sincerity and spirit. He was an elderly gentlemen from the Arabs of the south.

35. DHARGHAMA IBN MALIK

Shaykh Al-Tousi[119] and Ibn Shahr Ashoub[120] mention Dharghama amongst the list of companions killed in the first offensive of the battle of Karbala. He is also mentioned in Al-Ziyara[121] and Al-Rajabiya. According to the sources, he has not been affiliated with any tribe. No details about his background are reported.

36. 'AABIS IBN ABI SHABIB AL-SHAKIRI

'Aabis is mentioned by Al-Tabari,[122] Shaykh Al-Tousi,[123] Al-Khawarizmi,[124] and Al-Ziyara.[125] He is also mentioned in Al-Rajabiya as "Ibn Shabib." 'Aabis was amongst the greatest men of his time. In sincerity and spirit he was top amongst the revolutionaries. 'Aabis was a leader, a brave soul, an outspoken warrior, and a deeply spiritual man. He was wise and prudent. In a discussion with Muslim ibn 'Aqeel, he noted his skepticism of the people in their dedication to supporting the Imam's (a) movement. It did not falter his commitment, his devotion to the revolution was unwavering.[126]

Muslim ibn 'Aqeel sent 'Aabis with the letter to Imam Hussain (a) informing the Imam (a) of the Kufans' allegiance to him. That letter also called on the Imam (a) to come forward to Iraq. This, of course, was before the coup against Muslim in Kufa.

Al-Shakiri referred to his lineage and belonging to the clan of Shakir, which was part of tribe of Jutham. They were from the Qahtan bloodline. 'Aabis was a prominent figure who settled in Kufa, but was originally from Yemen. He was of southern Arab descent.

37. 'AMER IBN HASSAAN IBN SHURAYH AL-TAA'I

Al-Najashi mentions 'Amer in the biography of his grandson, Ahmad ibn 'Amer. He describes that 'Amer, "was killed with Hussain ibn Ali (a) in Karbala."[127] Shaykh Al-Tousi mentions him as "Ammar ibn Hassaan ibn Shurayh Al-Taa'i."[128] He is also mentioned in Al-Ziyara[129] and in Al-Rajabiya. Ibn Shahr Ashoub mentions him as one of the companions martyred in the first offensive of the battle.[130] 'Amer accompanied Imam Hussain (a) on his journey to Iraq from its outset in Mecca. He was a southern Arab who hailed from Yemen.

The information provided in the sources is limited to this.

38. 'AMER IBN MUSLIM

Al-Ziyara and Al-Rajabiya mention him in this manner.[131] Ibn Shahr Ashoub considers him amongst the companions that were killed in the first offensive of the battle.[132] Shaykh Al-Tousi mentions him as well, but notes that he was unknown.[133] Sayyid Al-Ameen attributed a lineage to him with, "Al-'Abdi." Bahreluloom attributed a lineage to him in commentary on Rijal Al-Shaykh with, "Al-Sa'di." Both lineages are from the bloodline of 'Adnan. Moreover, 'Amer was a northern Arab from Basra.

The information provided in the sources is limited to this.

39. ABDUL-RAHMAN IBN ABDULLAH IBN AL-KUDAR (AL-KUDAN) AL-ARHABI

He is mentioned by Al-Tabari as "Al-Kudan"[134] and by Ibn Shahr Ashoub as "Al-Kudar." They both consider him amongst the fallen martyrs of the first offensive in the battle of Karbala.[135] Al-Ziyara[136] and Shaykh Al-Tousi[137] mention him as well. Abdul-Rahman was one of the message carriers of Kufa to Imam Hussain (a).[138] He was in Kufa with Muslim ibn 'Aqeel during his stay there. Arhab was a large tribe from Hamadan. They were of the Qahtan bloodline. Abdul-Rahman was a southern Arab originally from Yemen.

40. ABDUL-RAHMAN IBN ABED-RABBUH AL-ANSARI AL-KHAZRAJI

He is mentioned by Al-Tabari[139] and Shaykh Al-Tousi,[140] who cited his lineage to Al-Khazraj. He is also mentioned in Bihar

Al-Anwar.[141] Ibn Tawous mentions him as one of the individuals who would take people's allegiance to Imam Hussain (a). Abdul-Rahman was one of the prominent personalities in Kufan society. He was a southern Arab originally from Yemen.

The information provided in the sources is limited to this.

41. ABDUL-RAHMAN IBN ABDULLAH AL-YAZNI

This Abdul-Rahman is mentioned by Ibn Shahr Ashoub,[142] Al-Khawarizmi,[143] and Bihar Al-Anwar.[144] We find it plausible that he is the same individual mentioned in Al-Rajabiya as "Abdul-Rahman ibn Abdullah Al-Azdi," in disagreement with Sayyid Al-Khoei who consolidated him with the other mentioned name "Abdul-RAhman ibn Abdullah ibn Al-Kudan Al-Arhabi."[145] Al-Yazni refers to being from the tribe of Yazn, which belongs to Humayr. Abdul-Rahman was a southern Arab from Yemen.

The information provided in the sources is limited to this.

42. ABDUL-RAHMAN IBN 'URWA AL-GHAFARI

He is mentioned by Al-Khawarizmi[146] and Bihar Al-Anwar.[147] Perhaps he is one of the Ghafari brothers, sons of 'Urza ibn Huraq. The reason we raise this possibility instead of postulating him to be someone else is the fact that Al-Khawarizmi and Muhammad ibn Abi Talib Al-Mousawi, who is cited by Al-Majlisi in Bihar Al-Anwar, mention the two Ghafari brothers after mentioning this particular individual. All of the sources speak of the Ghafari brothers together. They say that the brothers sought permission from Imam Hussain (a) to enter the battlefield, together. They fought and died on the battlefield, together. None of the sources speak of them separately. This particular Ghafari was mentioned in two different places by Al-Khawarizmi and Al-Majlisi in Bihar. A line of poetry was attributed to him in which he said, "Truly Banu Ghafar have come to know…"

Al-Ghafari is a reference to being from the clan of Ghafar ibn Mulayl, from the Kinana tribe. They were of the 'Adnan bloodline. Al-Ghafari was a northern Arab.

43. ABUL-RAHMAN IBN 'URZA IBN HURAQ AL-GHAFARI

This Abdul-Rahman is mentioned by Al-Tabari,[148] Shaykh Al-Tousi,[149] Al-Khawarizmi,[150] and Al-Rajabiya. He is also mentioned in Bihar Al-Anwar and Al-Ziyara, except that in it he is referred to within the phrase, "the sons of 'Urwa ibn Huraq."[151] His grandfather, Huraq, was one of the companions of the Commander of the Faithful Imam Ali (a). He fought alongside Imam Ali (a) in the battles of Jamal, Siffin, and Nahrawan. Though a young man, Abdul-Rahman was one of the noble men of Kufa. He was a northern Arab.

44. ABDULLAH IBN 'URZA IBN HURAQ AL-GHAFARI

Abdullah is mentioned in the same sources as his brother above. In those sources, he is notably discussed with the same features as his brother Abdul-Rahman ibn 'Urza ibn Huraq Al-Ghafari.

45. ABDULLAH IBN 'UMAYR AL-KALBI

He is mentioned by Al-Tabari[152] and Ibn Shahr Ashoub as one of the companions killed in the first offensive of the battle. He is also referred to as "Abdullah ibn 'Umayr."[153] In addition, Al-Khawarizmi,[154] Bihar Al-Anwar,[155] Al-Ziyara,[156] and Al-Rajabiya include him in their lists of companions who were with Imam Hussain (a) in Karbala.

Abdullah was from the Banu 'Aleem tribe. After seeing that Ibn Ziyad was mobilizing forces in Kufa to send to fight Imam Hussain (a), Abdullah left towards the Imam (a) with his wife Um Wahab bint Abed, who was from the lineage of Al-Nimr ibn Qasit. Abdullah was the second martyr from the companions of Imam Hussain (a). His wife was killed shortly after his death, struck on the head by one the Umayyad soldiers as she was mourning of the body of her martyred husband.

Abdullah was a young man. He was a fierce fighter and considered as one of the greatest revolutionaries in spirit and morale. Abdullah's tribe was from Kinanah, which belongs to the Quda'a. The title Al-Kalbi refers to the people of Kalb who also belonged to Quda'a. They were of the Qahtan bloodline. Abdullah was a southern Arab, originally from Yemen.

46. ABDULLAH IBN YAZID IBN NABEET (THABEET) AL-'ABDI

Abdullah is mentioned by Al-Tabari[157] and Ibn Shahr Ashoub as one of the companions killed in the first offensive of the battle;[158] expect that he is referred to as "Ibn Yazid." In Al-

Ziyara[159] and Al-Rajabiya, it mentions him with his father and brother: "Peace be upon Badr ibn Raqeet and his sons Abdullah and Ubaydallah." Abdullah left Basra with his father yazid ibn Nabeet when the Basrawis called on Imam Hussain (a) to come to Iraq as they were ready to support him.[160] His title, Al-'Abdi, refers to his lineage to the tribe of 'Abdel-Qays. He is from the 'Adnan bloodline. Abdullah was a young northern Arab from Basra.

47. UBAYDALLAH IBN YAZID IBN NABEET (THA-BEET) AL-'ABDI

Ubaydallah is mentioned in the same sources as his brother above. In those sources, he is notably discussed with the same features as his brother Abdullah ibn Yazid ibn Nabeet (Thabeet) Al-'Abdi.

48. IMRAN IBN KA'B IBN HARITH AL-ASHJA'I

He is mentioned by Ibn Shar Ashoub as one of the companions that were martyred in the first offensive of the battle.[161] Shaykh Al-Tousi recalls him as "Imran ibn Ka'b."[162] In Al-Rajabiya he is referred to as "Umar ibn Abi Ka'b." Apparently they are all in reference to the same one and the discrepancy being typographical errors in relating the narrations. Imran belonged to the Ashja' tribe which was from Ghatflan. Their lineage goes to Qays 'Aylan and the bloodline of 'Adnan. Imran was a northern Arab. No other details about his background are reported.

49. Ammar ibn Abi Salama al-Dalani

Ammar is mentioned by Ibn Shar Ashoub as one of the companions that were martyred in the first offensive of the battle.[163] He is also cited in Al-Ziyara but as "Al-Hamadani."[164] Al-Dalani comes from the Hamadan tribe of the Qahtan bloodline. They were southern Arabs that were originally from Yemen but settled in Kufa.

50. Ammar ibn Hassaan ibn Shurayh al-Tafi

Ammar has been mentioned in Al-Ziyara, as well as in Al-Rajabiya by "Ammar ibn Hassaan."

51. Amr ibn Junada ibn al-Harith al-Ansari

He is mentioned by Ibn Shahr Ashoub,[165] Al-Khawarizmi,[166] and Al-Bihar.[167] We believe that this is the Amr that after his father was killed in battle, his mother ordered him to go forward and fight for the Imam (a). When he came forward, Imam Hussain (a) disfavored the idea of granting him permission. He said, "This is a young man whose father was just killed. His mother would detest him going into the battlefield [now]…" Amr replied, "It is my mother who ordered me to do so…"[168] It only seems reasonable that this incident did not happen twice, since both individuals supposedly had the exact same stories told about them. At the same time in the other story that is reported, we don't know the name of the son or the father. Is it Umar or Umayr ibn Kanad that is being referred to in Al-Rajabiya? Thus, we find it most probable that the story is about Amr here. Moreover, Amr was a young southern Arab from Yemen.

52. UMAR IBN JUNDUB AL-HADRAMI

He is mentioned in Al-Ziyara[169] as such and in another edition as "Ibn Al-Ahdouth." Al-Hadrami refers to being form the Hadhramowt, a tribe from the Qahtan bloodline. Or it is a reference to being from the Banu Hadrami tribe, one of the tribes of Yemen. They were southern Arabs originally from Yemen. No other details about his background are reported.

53. AMR IBN KHALID AL-AZDI

He is mentioned by Ibn Shahr Ashoub,[170] Bihar Al-Anwar,[171] and Al-Khawarizmi.[172] Al-Tustari concluded in Qamous Al-Rijal that Amr here is the same as "Umar ibn Khalid Al-Saydawi," arguing that "Al-Azdi" is a typographical error from "Al-Asadi." At first we would have leaned towards the same conclusion before reviewing Al-Tustari's book; however, we have found it to be more probable that they are indeed different persons, even though the possibility of Al-Tustari mentions is existent. Amr was from the Azd tribe. He was a southern Arab from Yemen. No other details about his background are reported.

54. UMAR IBN KHALID AL-SAYDAWI

Umar here is mentioned by Al-Tabari,[173] Al-Ziyara,[174] Bihar Al-Anwar,[175] and Al-Khawarizmi.[176] In Al-Rajabiya, he is mentioned as "Amr ibn Khalaf" which is seemingly a typographical deviation from "Khalid." Umar belonged to the

Sayda' clan which was from the Asad tribe. Northern Arabs, they are of the 'Adnan bloodline.

55. AMR IBN ABDULLAH AL-JUNDA'I

He is mentioned by Ibn Shahr Ashoub amongst the companions that were killed in the first offensive.[177] Amr was also mentioned in Al-Ziyara.[178] Al-Junda'i referred to being from the clan of Junda' ibn Malik, which belonged to the Hamadan tribe. They were southern Arabs from Yemen.

56. AMR IBN DHABEE'A AL-DHABA'I

Amr is mentioned by Shaykh Al-Tousi[179] and Ibn Shahr Ashoub as one of the companions martyred in the first offensive of the battle. Ibn Shahr Ashoub refers to him as "Umar ibn Mashee'a."[180] He is also mentioned in Al-Ziyara,[181] as well as in Al-Rajabiya as "Dhabee'a ibn Umar" mistakenly switching the name and lineage. His name Al-Dhaba'i is a reference to his lineage from Dhaba' ibn Wabara who is from the bloodline of Qahtan. Amr is a southern Arab from Yemen.

57. AMR IBN QARADHA IBN KA'B AL-ANSARI

He is mentioned by Al-Tabari,[182] Ibn Shahr Ashoub,[183] Al-Ziyara,[184] Bihar Al-Anwar, and Al-Khawarizmi.[185] Al-Ziyara refers to him as "Umar ibn Ka'b Al-Ansari," and in another edition as "Imran" as well as the name listed here. Al-Rajabiya cites to this name as well. Amr was sent by Imam Hussain (a) as a negotiator to Umar ibn Saad to try to stop the Umayyads from persisting on aggression. Amr was a southern Arab from Yemen.

58. UMAR IBN ABDULLAH (ABU THUMAMA) AL-SAA'IDI

Al-Ziyara,[186] Al-Tabari,[187] Ibn Shahr Ashoub,[188] and Al-Rajabiya mention Umar. He is mentioned in Al-Rijal as "Amr ibn Thumama." Al-Khawarizmi[189] recalls him as "Abu Thumama Al-Saydawi," which is also what he is referred to as in Bihar Al-Anwar.[190] Umar ibn Abdullah was responsible for collecting money from the people of Kufa during Muslim ibn Aqeel's presence there. He was also tasked with buying the weaponry for the supporters of the Imam (a). He was an Arabian knight and a prominent Shia personality.[191] Muslim ibn 'Aqeel assigned a quarter of the tribes of Tameem and Hamadan under his authority during Muslim's short movement against Ubaydallah ibn Ziyad in Kufa. Al-Saa'idi belonged to the Hamadan tribe. They were southern Arabs originally from Yemen.

59. AMR IBN MOUTTAA' AL-JU'FI

Amr here is mentioned by Ibn Shahr Ashoub,[192] Bihar Al-Anwar,[193] and Al-Khawarizmi.[194] He was a southern Arab from Yemen.

60. UMAYR IBN ABDULLAH AL-MUTHHIJI

Umayr is mentioned by Ibn Shahr Ashoub,[195] Al-Khawarizmi,[196] and Bihar Al-Anwar.[197] Muthhij is from the Kahlan tribe which belongs to the Qahtan bloodline. He was a southern Arab from Yemen.

61. Qarib the Servant of Imam Hussain (a)

He has been mentioned in Al-Ziyara.[198]

62. Qasit ibn Zuhayr (Thuhayr) Al-Taghlibi

Qasit is mentioned in Al-Ziyara[199] and Al-Rajabiya. Ibn Shahr Ashoub mentions him amongst the companions that were killed in the first offensive of the battle of Karbala.[200] Shaykh Al-Tousi[201] also mentions him but by the name "Qasit ibn Abdullah." His lineage goes back to the tribe of Taghlib ibn Wael, which is a tribe from the bloodline of 'Adnan. They were northern Arabs.

63. Qasim ibn Habib Al-Azdi

Qasim has been mentioned in Al-Ziyara[202] and by Shaykh Al-Tousi.[203] He has also been mentioned in Al-Rajabiya as "Qasim ibn Habib," as well as "Al-Qasim ibn Al-Harith Al-Kahili" which we believe is most likely a typographical deviation from the first name. Qasim was a southern Arab from Yemen.

64. Qura ibn Abi Qura Al-Ghafari

Ibn Shahr Ashoub,[204] Al-Khawarizmi,[205] and Bihar Al-Anwar[206] mention Qura. In Al-Rajabiya of the Bihar edition he is referred to as "Uthman ibn Farwa Al-Ghafari," while in the Iqbal edition he is said to be "Uthman ibn 'Urwa Al-Ghafari." Al-Ghafari belonged to the bloodline of 'Adnan. He was a northern Arab.

65. QA'NAB IBN AMR AL-NIMRI

Qa'nab is referred to as "Al-Timri" in Al-Ziyara.[207] Al-Nimr ibn Fasit was from the bloodline of 'Adnan. They were Arabs of the north.

66. KARDOUS (KARESH) IBN ZUHAYR (THUHAYR) AL-TAGHLIBI

Kardous is mentioned in the same sources as his brother above. In those sources, he is notably discussed with the same features as his brother Qasit ibn Zuhayr (Thuhayr) Al-Taghlibi.

67. KUNANAH IBN 'ATEEQ AL-TAGHLIBI

Kunanah is mentioned in Al-Ziyara[208] and Al-Rajabiya. Ibn Shahr Ashoub mentions him amongst the companions that were killed in the first offensive of the battle of Karbala.[209] Shaykh Al-Tousi[210] also mentions him. His lineage goes back to the tribe of Taghlib ibn Wael, which is a tribe from the bloodline of 'Adnan. They were northern Arabs.

68. MALIK IBN ABED IBN SAREE' AL-JABIRI

Malik is mentioned in the same sources as his brother above. In those sources, he is notably discussed with the same features as his brother Sayf ibn Al-Harith ibn Suraye' Al-Jabiri. In Al-Rajabiya he is addressed as "Malik ibn Abdullah Al-Jabiri."

69. MAJMA' IBN ABDULLAH AL-'AA'ITHI AL-MUTHHIJI

He is mentioned by Al-Tabari[211] and Ibn Shahr Ashoub as one of the companions that was martyred in the first offensive of the battle.[212] He is also mentioned in Al-Ziyara[213] and Al-

Rajabiya. Muthhij is from the Kahlan tribe, which belongs to the Qahtan bloodline. They were southern Arabs from Yemen.

70 & 71. MAS'OUD IBN AL-HAJJAJ AND HIS SON

They were both mentioned together in Al-Ziyara.[214] The father alone was mentioned in Al-Rajabiya. Ibn Shahr Ashoub mentions the father amongst the counted martyrs from the first offensive of the battle.[215]

72. MUSLIM IBN 'AWSAJA AL-ASADI

All of the sources recall Muslim ibn 'Awsaja Al-Asadi. He was the first martyr from the companions of Imam Hussain (a) after the first offensive of the battle.[216] Muslim was one of the companions of the Holy Prophet (s) who also narrated from the Prophet (s) himself. He would take people's allegiance for Imam Hussain (a). Muslim ibn 'Aqeel assigned a quarter of the tribes of Muthhij and Asad under his authority during Ibn 'Aqeel's short movement against Ubaydallah ibn Ziyad in Kufa. An elderly man, Muslim ibn 'Awsaja was great personality from the Asad tribe. He was also a prominent figure in greater Kufan society.

The Umayyad soldier Shabeth ibn Rib'i killed him, to which Shabeth expressed remorse afterwards. Muslim's title, Al-Asadi, signified his belonging to the Asad tribe which was from the bloodline of 'Adnan. He was a northern Arab.

73. MUSLIM IBN KATHEER AL-AZDI AL-A'RAJ

Shaykh Al-Tousi[217] and Ibn Shahr Ashoub record him in the list of companions that were killed in the first offensive of the battle of Karbala.[218] He is also mentioned in Al-Ziyara as "Aslem ibn Katheer Al-Azdi"[219] and in Al-Rajabiya as "Sulayman ibn Katheer." I believe they are the same individual. Al-Azdi refers to belonging to the tribe of Azd. Muslim was a southern Arab from Yemen.

74. MUNJIH THE SERVANT OF IMAM HUSSAIN (A)

In Qamous Al-Rijal, Al-Tustari said, Relaying from Rabee' Al-Abrar by Al-Zumkhishri, that his mother ("Um Munjih") was a follower of Imam Hussain (a). Initially she was a slave. Imam Hussain (a) bought her from Nawfal ibn Al-Harith ibn Abdul-Muttalib, and then married her to Sahm "Abu Mujih" and they begot Munjih."[220] Munjih is mentioned by Al-Tabari,[221] Shaykh Al-Tousi,[222] Al-Ziyara,[223] and Al-Rajabiya.

75. NAFI' IBN HILAL AL-JAMELI

He is mentioned by Al-Tabari,[224] Shaykh Al-Tousi,[225] Al-Ziyara as "Al-Bajeli" as a typographical error.[226] The same is mentioned in Ibn Shahr Ashoub's Manaqib.[227] Al-Rajabiya mentions him without a title of lineage. Nafi' helped Al-Abbas ibn Ali (a) in retrieving water for the camp of Imam Hussain (a). He was a prominent figure in Kufa. The title Al-Jameli refers to being from the tribe of Jamel ibn Saad, which is from Muthhij. They were southern Arabs originally from Yemen.

76. NU'MAN IBN AMR AL-RASIBI

He is mentioned by Ibn Shahr Ashoub as one of the companions that was killed in the first offensive of the battle of Karbala.[228] He is also mentioned by Shaykh,[229] as well as in Al-Rajabiya but without a title of lineage. Rasib belongs to the Azd tribe. They hail from Yemen and are southern Arabs.

77. NA'EEM IBN 'AJALAN AL-ANSARI

Ibn Shahr Ashoub recalls him amongst the companions that were martyred in the first offensive of the battle.[230] Shaykh Al-Tousi mentions Na'eem.[231] He is also mentioned in Al-Ziyara,[232] as well as in Al-Rajabiya but without a title of lineage. Na'eem was a southern Arab from Yemen.

78. WAHAB IBN ABDULLAH JANAB AL-KALBI

Ibn Shahr Ashoub mentions him as "Wahab ibn Abdullah Al-Kalbi,"[233] while Al-Khawarizmi refers to him as "Wahab ibn Abdullah ibn Janab Al-Kalbi."[234] He is also mentioned in Bihar Al-Anwar.[235] The sources say that his wife and mother were present with him in Karbala. Some of the sources indicate that his wife was killed. Al-Khawarizmi says that the one was killed was actually his mother. Some of the sources also say that his name was Wahab ibn Wahab, and that he was originally Christian and became Muslim. Ibn Shahr Ashoub describes that he was taken as a prisoner of war and not killed, while other sources state that he was in fact martyred.

We find it to be highly likely that this Wahab is the son of Um Wahab and Abdullah ibn 'Umayr ibn Janab Al-Kalbi, whom we discussed earlier. It was his father's wife, Um Wahab – his mother, that was killed while she mourned over his dead body. Thus, Al-Khawarizmi would be correct in his record that it was Wahab's mother, not wife, that was killed in Karbala. Wahab was a young southern Arab who settled in Kufa. He is originally from Yemen.

79. YAHYA IBN SALEEM AL-MAZINI

He is mentioned by Ibn Shahr Ashoub[236] and Al-Khawarizmi.[237]

80. YAZID IBN AL-HUSSEYN AL-HAMADANI AL-MASHRIQI AL-QAREE

Shaykh Al-Tousi mentions him in his book.[238] He is also listed in Al-Ziyara.[239] Yazid ibn Al-Husseyn was a southern Arab from Yemen.

81. YAZID IBN ZIYAD IBN MUHASIR ABU AL-SHA'SHA' AL-KINDI

He is mentioned by Al-Tabari,[240] Ibn Shahr Ashoub,[241] Al-Khawarizmi,[242] and in Al-Ziyara as "Ibn Al-Muthahir."[243] Some of the sources mistakenly refer to him as "Ibn Muhajir." Al-Tabari's story is conflicting with regards to Yazid ibn Ziyad. In one part Al-Tabari says that Yazid ibn Ziyad switched to the camp of Imam Hussain (a) from the Umayyad army after the Umayyad generals had refused Imam Hussain's (a) overtures. In another part he says that Yazid ibn Ziyad went out to support Imam Hussain (a) from Kufa before Imam Hussain (a) was stopped by Al-Hur. The same conflict is found in what is relayed by Sayyid Al-Ameen.[244] Yazid ibn Ziyad was a southern Arab who settled in Kufa but was originally from Yemen.

82. YAZID IBN NABEET (THABEET AL-'ABDI)

Yazid is mentioned by Al-Tabari,[245] as well as being cited as in Al-Ziyara but as "Yazid ibn Thabeet Al-Qaysi."[246] He is also mentioned in Al-Rajabiya by the name "Badr ibn Raqeet." Sayyid Al-Khoei addresses him by the name "Badr ibn Raqeed."[247]

After Imam Hussain's (a) letter reached the nobles of Basra, Yazid ibn Nabeet came to Imam Hussain (a) with his sons, Abdullah and Ubaydallah, from Basra to Mecca. Yazid was part of a group of Shia living in Basra. Al-'Abdi referred to his belonging to the tribe of 'Abdel-Qays. They were Arabs of the north.

Presumably Amongst the Martyrs of Karbala

1. IBRAHIM IBN AL-HUSSEYN AL-AZDI

He is mentioned by Ibn Shahr Ashoub.[1] There is some poetry narrated in the sources that is attributed to him, but we find that is most probably fabricated. Ibrahim is also mentioned by Sayyid Al-Ameen in A'yan Al-Shia. He belongs to the bloodline of 'Adnan. He is a northern Arab. Nothing else of his background is reported in the sources.

2. ABU AMR AL-NAHSHALI OR AL-KHATH'AMI

Ibn Nama Al-Hilli describes him as being, "a devout believer who prayed very much."[2] Al-Majlisi mentions him in Bihar Al-Anwar, narrating from Ibn Nama. Sayyid Al-Ameen also mentions him in A'yan Al-Shia but refers to him as "Abu 'Amer Al-Nahshali."

Is he the same person as "Shabib ibn Abdullah Al-Nahshali" that we discussed previously? In Mutheer Al-Ahzan, Ibn Nama says that Abu Amr was killed in a duel during the battle of

Karbala. Ibn Shahr Ashoub says that Shabib was killed in the first offensive. This would lead to the conclusion that they were two different individuals. However, the fact that Ibn Nama mentions Abu Amr Al-Nahshali without mentioning Shabib, and that the other sources neglected to mention Amr but all mention Shabib pushes us to conclude that they were indeed the same person.

Al-Nahshali refers to being from the clan of Nahshal ibn Da-rim, who belonged to the tribe of Tamim. They were northern Arabs from the bloodline of 'Adnan.

3. HAMMAD IBN HAMMAD AL-KHUZA'I AL-MURADI

This is the manner in which his name was relayed in Bihar Al-Anwar's version of Al-Rajabiya.[3] In the Iqbal version of Al-Rajabiya, "Al-Khuza'i" is not mentioned. Sayyid Al-Khoei also includes his name in Mu'jam Al-Rijal.[4] However, we doubt that he was indeed a factual person in history because we cast doubt on any name that was only mentioned in Al-Rajabiya and not mentioned in any place else.

4. HANTHALA IBN AMR AL-SHAYBANI

Ibn Shahr Ashoub mentions him as one of the companions that were killed in the first offensive of the battle of Karbala.[5] He is also mentioned by Sayyid Al-Ameen. Sayyid Al-Khoei elected that Hanthala here was the same as "Hanthala ibn As'ad Al-Shabami."[6] Al-Tustari elected the same opinion. We find this to be unlikely, however, given that Al-Shaybani was killed in the first offensive, while all the sources that mention Al-Shabami say he was killed in a duel during the battle. Al-Shaybani is a title referring to the Shayban tribe. They are northern Arabs from the bloodline of 'Adnan.

5. RUMAYTH IBN AMRO

Shaykh Al-Tousi mentions Rumayth without particularly pointing to his martyrdom. He is also mentioned in Al-Rajabiya. Sayyid Al-Khoei discusses him without referencing Al-Rajabiya.[7]

6. ZAI'DA IBN MUHAJIR

He is mentioned in Al-Rajabiya. Is it possible that he is a typographical deviation from the already mentioned companion, "Yazid ibn Ziyad ibn Al-Muhajir (Al-Muthahir)"?

7. ZUHAYR IBN SAI'B

Zuhayr is mentioned in Al-Rajabiya. Sayyid Al-Khoei cites to Al-Rajabiya with reference to Zuhayr.[8] In the Iqbal edition of Al-Rajabiya he is mentioned as "Zuhayr ibn Sayyar."

8. ZUHAYR IBN SULAYMAN

He is mentioned in the Bihar version of Al-Rajabiya as "Zuhayr ibn Salman." Sayyid Al-Khoei also mentions him in his book citing to Al-Rajabiya.[9]

9. ZUHAYR IBN SALEEM AL-AZDI

This Zuhayr is mentioned in Al-Ziyara. Ibn Shahr Ashoub lists him as one of the companions that were martyred in the first offensive of the battle. We lean towards uniting him with the "Zuhayr ibn Bishr Al-Khath'ami" who was mentioned before, because of the discrepancy found between the two versions of Al-Ziyara in Al-Bihar and Al-Iqbal. It is more probable that his name actually was "Zuhayr ibn Bishr" rather than "Zuhayr ibn Saleem," with regards to historical accuracy, because of it appearing in Al-Rajabiya as such as well.

10. SALMAN IBN MUDHARIB AL-BUJALI

Al-Khawarizmi mentions him as being Zuhayr ibn Al-Qayn's cousin. Al-Khawarizmi says that he went towards the camp of Imam Hussain (a) with his cousin Zuhayr before they reached Karbala.[10] Sayyid Al-Khoei also mentions him but without a reference.[11] Al-Bujali is a title referring to his lineage from Bujayla. They are southern Arabs from Yemen.

11. SULAYMAN IBN SULAYMAN AL-AZDI

He is mentioned in Al-Rajabiya.

12. SULAYMAN IBN 'AOUN AL-HADRAMI

He is mentioned in Al-Rajabiya.

13. SULAYMAN IBN KATHEER

He is mentioned in Al-Rajabiya. We find it more probable that he is the same person as "Muslim ibn Katheer Al-Azdi Al-A'raj" who we discussed previously.

14. AMER IBN JULAYDA (KHULAYDA)

He is mentioned in Al-Rajabiya.

15. AMER IBN MALIK

He is mentioned in Al-Rajabiya.

16. Abdul-Rahman ibn Yazid

He is mentioned in Al-Rajabiya.

17. 'Uthman ibn Farwa ('Urwa) Al-Ghafari

He is mentioned in Al-Rajabiya. We find it more probable that he is the same person as "Qurra ibn Qurra Al-Ghafari."

18. 'Umar ('Umayr) ibn Kannad

He is mentioned in Al-Rajabiya.

19. Abdullah ibn Abi Bakr

Sayyid Al-Ameen said, "Al-Jahith said in Kitab Al-Hayawan, 'He is a martyr from the martyrs of the day of *Taf* [Ashura]. I was not able to access a copy of Kitab Al-Hayawan for me to confirm this. It is possible that Al-Jahith had meant to say that Abdullah ibn Abi Bakr was one of the companions that was killed in the revolution of Ibrahim ibn Abdullah, martyred in Bakhamra, during the reign of Abi Ja'far Al-Mansour in Basra.

20. Abdullah ibn 'Urwa Al-Ghafari

Ibn Shahr Ashoub mentions him as one of the companions that were killed in the first offensive of the battle of Karbala.[12] Al-Tustari proposed strongly that this Abdullah was the same as "Abdullah ibn 'Urza ibn Huraq Al-Ghafari."[13] We think otherwise. The two Ghafari brothers, the sons of Huraq, are mentioned in the sources as having fought in duels – not in the first offensive. They fought and died together. Al-Khawarizmi clearly states this before mentioning them by saying, "And the following people are those who remained for the duels of the battle."[14] Unlike what Ibn Shahr Ashoub has mentioned of this Abdullah, the sons of Huraq were not in the first offensive. The sources show us, in fact, that they were most likely of the last men to be martyred in amongst the companions. This is with indication to what seems to be a real chronological order given by the sources when the say: he went out and fought, then so and so followed, and then so and so came forward, etc. Nonetheless, we find it unlikely that this Abdullah was an actual historical person when it comes down to it, because he is only mentioned by Ibn Shahr Ashoub.

21. GHAYLAN IBN ABDUL-RAHMAN

He is mentioned in Al-Rajabiya.

22. AL-QASIM IBN AL-HARITH AL-KAMAHELI

He is mentioned in Al-Rajabiya. Is it possible that he is the same person as the already mentioned companion, "Qasim ibn Habib Al-Azdi"?

23. QAYS IBN ABDULLAH AL-HAMADANI

He is mentioned in Al-Rajabiya.

24. MALIK IBN DAWDAN

Malik is mentioned Ibn Shahr Ashoub.[15] Dawdan belonged to the tribe of Asad ibn Khuzayman. They were form the bloodline of 'Adnan. Malik was a northern Arab.

25. MUSLIM IBN KANNAD

He is mentioned in Al-Rajabiya.

26. MUSLIM THE SERVANT OF 'AMER IBN MUSLIM

He is mentioned in Al-Rajabiya.

27. MUNEE' IBN ZIYAD

He is mentioned in Al-Rajabiya.

28. NU'MAN IBN AMRO

He is mentioned in Al-Rajabiya.

29. YAZID IBN MUHAJIR AL-JU'FI

Al-Khawarizmi mentions him in Maqtal Al-Hussain.[16] We propose that he is the same person as "Yazid ibn Ziyad ibn Muhasir Abu Al-Sha'sha' Al-Kindi" that has been mentioned previously. The title Al-Ju'fi was a reference to being from the tribe of Ju'fi ibn Saad. They belong to the greater tribe of Saad, which is from Muthhij. They are of the bloodline of Qahtan. Yazid was a southern Arab from Yemen.

THE COMPANIONS MARTYRED IN KUFA

1. ABDEL-A'LA IBN YAZID AL-KALBI

Abdel-A'la was an Arab of the south. He was a young Kufan who paid allegiance to Muslim ibn 'Aqeel upon his arrival to Kufa. Abdel-A'la quickly got up in arms when Muslim ibn 'Aqeel announced his movement after Hani ibn 'Urwa was captured. Abdel-A'la went to follow Muslim in the neighborhood of Bani Fatayan. He was captured, however, by Katheer ibn Shehab ibn Al-Husseyn Al-Harithi of Muthhij. Ubaydallah ibn Ziyad had ordered him to arrest and capture any persons from Muthhij that followed Muslim ibn 'Aqeel. He wanted to unearth any support Muslim had garnered.

Katheer took Abdel-A'la to Ubaydallah ibn Ziyad. Abdel-A'la claimed that he had wished to join Ibn Ziyad. Ibn Ziyad did not believe him and ordered that he be imprisoned.[1] When Ibn Ziyad had Muslim ibn 'Aqeel and Hani ibn 'Urwa executed, he summoned Abdel-A'la to come forth. Ibn Ziyad said, "Tell me

119

your story." "I went out to see what the people were up to, and then Katheer ibn Shehab arrested me," Abdel-A'la replied. "Swear that you had no motive but that which you mentioned!" Abdel-A'la would not swear. "Take him to the Sabee' cemetery and off with his head!" Abdel-A'la was taken and executed.[2]

2. ABDULLAH IBN BAQTUR

Abdullah was a southern Arab from the Humayri tribe. His mother was a caretaker of Imam Hussain (a). Ibn Hijr mentions him in Al-'Isaba, in which he said that he was a companion of Imam Hussain (a). Al-Husseyn ibn Numayr arrested him on his way to deliver a message to Imam Hussain (a) who had already left Mecca and was making his way to Muslim ibn 'Aqeel. Ubaydallah ibn Ziyad had him executed and his body thrown from the rooftop of the palace. Though every bone in his body was broken, he did not die upon impact and was still breathing. Abdel-Malik ibn Umayr Al-Lukhami went down and finished him off.[3]

3. AMMARA IBN SALKHAB AL-AZDI

Ammara was a young southern Arab from Kufa. He joined the movement to support Muslim ibn 'Aqeel in Kufa. Soon after he was arrested and thrown in prison. After Muslim ibn 'Aqeel and Hani ibn 'Urwa were captured and executed, Ibn Ziyad called on Ammara. When he was brought before him Ibn Ziyad asked, "What tribe are you from?" He answered, "From the Azd tribe." "Take him to his people," Ibn Ziyad said. He wasn't set free. He was executed in front of his tribe.

4. QAYS IBN MUS-HIR AL-SAYDAWI

Qays was a young northern Arab who belonged to the Asad tribe and the 'Adnan bloodline. He lived in Kufa. He was noble amongst his tribesmen. Qays was one of the message carriers for the people of Kufa to Imam Hussain (a) after the Imam (a) refused to pay allegiance to Yazid and left Mecca. He carried a message from Muslim to Imam Hussain (a) informing the Imam (a) of those who paid allegiance and their calling for him to come to Iraq. He then carried the message of Imam Hussain (a) back to Kufa that informed the people that he was coming to Iraq. Qays was captured by Al-Husseyn ibn Numayr. Upon his capture, Qays rid himself of the letter. Husseyn brought Qays before Ubaydallah ibn Ziyad. Ibn Ziyad interrogated Qays to find out who were the Kufan men that sent letters to Imam Hussain (a). He was not able to get a name out of him. Ubaydallah sentenced him to death. He ordered his soldiers to take Qays to the top of the palace, execute him, and throw his body from the rooftop.[4]

5. MUSLIM IBN 'AQEEL IBN ABI TALIB

Muslim ibn 'Aqeel's mother was a woman from the Levant by the name of Hulya. His father was 'Aqeel, Imam Ali's (a) brother. Thus, Muslim was Imam Hussain's (a) first cousin. He was sent by Imam Hussain (a) to Kufa to receive the people's allegiance for the Imam (a). He left Mecca in the middle of the month of Ramadhan in 60 AH. Arriving in Kufa on the

6th of Shawwal, he was paid allegiance by eighteen thousand Kufans. Some sources say they were twenty-five thousand.

Ibn Ziyad was bent on quelling the movement that Muslim ibn 'Aqeel had invigorated. He was able to pinpoint the whereabouts of Muslim ibn 'Aqeel with the use of a spy. This spy was able to infiltrate the ranks of the revolutionaries by deceiving Muslim ibn 'Awsaja that he was a follower of Ahlulbayt (a). Ibn Ziyad had Hani ibn 'Urwa captured. Muslim was forced to announce his mobilization prematurely due to the circumstances. His forces besieged Ubaydallah ibn Ziyad in the royal palace, but it was too quickly that his forces dismantled and deserted their posts. Before he knew it, Muslim was alone. He sought refuge at the home of Madam Tawa'a who took him in. When her son, Bilal, knew that Muslim was staying in their home he sent word to Abdul-Rahman ibn Al-Ash'ath who informed Ibn Ziyad. Ubaydallah sent his soldiers to capture Muslim where he was staying. Muslim fought intensely against the Umayyad soldiers. He was finally captured with the increasing number of soldiers that encircled him. Ibn Ziyad ordered the execution of Muslim ibn 'Aqeel and Hani ibn 'Urwa. Their severed heads were dragged by horses in the markets of Kufa and taken as a tribute to Yazid ibn Mu'awiya.

6. HANI IBN 'URWA AL-MURADI

Hani ibn 'Urwa was a southern Arab from Muthhij. Regarded as one of the prominent Yemeni figures who settled in Kufa, he was also a companion of the Holy Prophet (s). Hani was one of the companions of the Commander of the Faithful Imam Ali (a) as well. He fought in the ranks of Imam Ali (a) in the battles of Jamal, Siffin, and Nahrawan. He was also one of the pillars of the movement of Hujr ibn 'Uday Al-Kindi against Ziyad ibn Abeeh.

Muslim ibn 'Aqeel stayed in Hani's home after Ubaydallah ibn Ziyad entered Kufa as its newly appointed Umayyad governor. Hani's involvement in the preparations for the revolution was revealed and was then arrested by Ibn Ziyad's men. Ibn Ziyad had him imprisoned and then executed, along with Muslim ibn 'Aqeel. Ibn Ziyad sent their decapitated heads to Damascus as tribute to Yazid.

Hani ibn 'Urwa was executed on the 8th of Thil-Hijja, 60 AH. That was the same day that Imam Hussain (a) left Mecca for his journey to Iraq. Hani was ninety years old.

THE HASHIMITE MARTYRS OF KARBALA

The narrations have differed on the total number of martyrs in Karbala, other than Imam Hussain (a), from the lineage of Ahlulbayt (a). Al-Mas'oudi states that there were thirteen martyrs from the Hashimites.[1] From our research we have found this to be the lowest number reported amongst the narrators on this account.

Al-Khawarizmi relates from Layth ibn Saad that fourteen Hashimites were martyred in Karbala.[2] Al-Khawarizmi mentions another narration relating it from Hassan Al-Basri, which states, "Hussain ibn Ali (a) was killed with sixteen members of his family – men that were unmatched by anyone on the face of the Earth."[3]

Al-Ziyara Al-Nahiya mentions a total of seventeen names, other than Imam Hussain (a). That number is in agreement with Shaykh Al-Mufid's findings. "The number of family members killed with Husssain (a) in the land of Karbala were

seventeen souls, and Hussain ibn Ali (a) was the eighteenth."[4]
These narrations are also in agreement, with regards to the
number they mention, with Al-Tabari. He counted the total
number of Hashimite martyrs to be nineteen, including Muslim ibn 'Aqeel and Abu Bakr ibn Ali ibn Abi Talib. He does
say that he is uncertain of Abu Bakr ibn Ali's death. Thus, his
total would be seventeen souls that were martyred in Karbala,
since Muslim was killed in Kufa. That is in direct agreement
with Al-Ziyara and Shaykh Al-Mufid. Al-Khawarizmi adds to
the agreement of the three narrations above with another narration related by Hassan Al-Basri. It states, "Hussain ibn Ali
(a) was killed with seventeen men from his family."[5]

Abul Faraj Al-Asfahani states, after displaying the names of
the Hashimite martyrs, "Those killed from the lineage of Abi
Talib, except those are contested, are a total of twenty two
men."[6] The names Abul Faraj listed include Imam Hussain (a)
and Muslim ibn 'Aqeel. As mentioned, Muslim was not killed
in Karbala but rather in Kufa. Thus, Abul-Faraj's total would
be twenty martyrs.

The greatest number of Hashimite martyrs in Karbala that our
study of the narrations has produced is twenty-five men. Al-
Khawarizmi relates, "The narrators have differed on the number of those killed on that day from the family of the pure
household. The greatest number being twenty seven..." He
includes the names after this, amongst them being Hussain ibn
Ali ibn Abi Talib (a) and Muslim ibn 'Aqeel ibn Abi Talib.[7]

Sayyid Muhsin Al-Ameen, may God rest his soul, wrote a table in A'yan Al-Shia for the total number of martyrs from the Hashimites. The heading of the table was, "The names we have gathered from the names of the Hashimite supporters of Imam Hussain (a) that were killed with him." In the table he listed thirty names. We don't know what references the Sayyid, may God rest his soul, relied on here.

THE NAMES OF THE HASHIMITE MARTYRS OF KARBALA

1. ALI IBN HUSSAIN AL-AKBAR

Ali Al-Akbar is discussed in Al-Ziyara, Al-Irshad, Al-Tabari, Al-Asfahani, Al-Khawarizmi, and Al-Mas'oudi. His kunya was Abul-Hassan. Some of the narrations say that he was twenty-seven years old and married.

His mother's name was Layla bint Abi Murra ibn 'Urwa ibn Mas'oud Al-Thaqafi. The son of Imam Hussain (a), Ali Al-Akbar was the first martyr from the Hashimites. He was killed by Murra ibn Munqith ibn Al-Nu'man Al-'Abdi.

2. ABDULLAH IBN ALI IBN ABI TALIB

Abdullah ibn Ali was named in Al-Ziyara, Al-Irshad, Al-Tabari, Al-Asfahani, Al-Mas'oudi, and Al-Khawarizmi. His mother was Ummul Baneen bint Huzam. Abdullah ibn Ali was twenty-five years old when he was killed. He had no children.

He was killed by Hani ibn Thabeet Al-Hadrami

3. JA'FAR IBN ALI IBN ABI TALIB

Ja'far ibn Ali is mentioned in Al-Ziyara, Al-Irshad, Al-Tabari, Al-Asfahani, Al-Mas'oudi, and Al-Khawarizmi. His mother was Ummul Baneen bint Huzam. He was nineteen years old when he was killed. Ja'far was killed by Hani ibn Thabeet Al-Hadrami or Khawle ibn Yazid Al-Asbahi.

4. UTHMAN IBN ALI IBN ABI TALIB

Utman ibn Ali is mentioned in Al-Ziyara, Al-Irshad, Al-Tabari, Al-Asfahani, Al-Mas'oudi, and Al-Khawarizmi. His mother was Ummul Baneen bint Huzam. He was twenty-one years old when he was killed. During the battle, Khawli ibn Yazid Al-Asbahi shot him with an arrow. The strike of the arrow weakened him. He was then attacked by an Umayyad soldier from the tribe of Aban ibn Darim. The Umayyad soldier killed Uthman ibn Ali and severed his head.

5. MUHAMMAD (AL-ASGHAR) IBN ALI IBN ABI TALIB

He is mentioned in Al-Ziyara, Al-Tabari, Al-Asfahani, and Al-Mas'oudi. His mother was said to be Asmaa' Bint 'Umays. Muhammad ibn Ali was killed by an Umayyad soldier from the tribe of Tamim.

6. ABBAS IBN ALI IBN ABI TALIB

Abbas ibn Ali is discussed in Al-Ziyara, Al-Irshad, Al-Tabari, Al-Asfahani, Al-Mas'oudi, and Al-Khawarizmi. He was the son of Ummul Baneen bint Huzam. His kunya was Abul-Fadl. He was the eldest of his brothers from the sons of Ummul

Baneen and the last of them to be martyred. Abbas ibn Ali was the flag-bearer of Imam Hussain (a).

He was killed by Zayd ibn Ruqad Al-Janbi and Hakim ibn Al-Tufayl Al-Taa'i, whom Al-Tabari refers to as Al-Sinbasi.

7. ABDULLAH IBN HUSSAIN IBN ALI IBN ABI TALIB

Abdullah ibn Hussain is mentioned in Al-Ziyara, Al-Irshad, Al-Tabari, Al-Asfahani, and Al-Khawarizmi. His mother was Rabab bint Imri' Al-Qays Al-Kalbi. Abdullah was a nursing baby when he was killed in the arms of his father Hussain (a). He was slaughtered by the arrow of 'Aqaba ibn Bishr. Al-Tabari states that the one who shot the arrow was Hani ibn Thabeet Al-Hadrami. Al-Ziyara states that it was Harmala ibn Kahil Al-Asadi.

8. ABU BAKR IBN HASSAN IBN ALI IBN ABI TALIB

He is mentioned in Al-Ziyara, Al-Irshad, Al-Tabari, Al-Asfahani, and Al-Mas'oudi. He was killed by Abdullah ibn 'Aqaba Al-Ghenwi or 'Aqaba Al-Ghenwi.

9. AL-QASIM IBN HASSAN IBN ALI IBN ABI TALIB

Al-Qasim is discussed in Al-Ziyara, Al-Irshad, Al-Tabari, Al-Asfahani, Al-Mas'oudi, and Al-Khawarizmi. He was Abu Bakr ibn Hassan's brother, from the same mother and father. Al-Qasim was killed by Amr ibn Saad ibn Nufayl Al-Azdi. In Al-Tabari, his killer's name is cited as Saad ibn Amr ibn Nufayl Al-Azdi.

10. ABDULLAH IBN HASSAN IBN ALI IBN ABI TALIB

He is mentioned in Al-Ziyara, Al-Irshad, Al-Tabari, Al-Asfahani, Al-Mas'oudi, and Al-Khawarizmi. Abdullah ibn Hassan was only eleven years old when he was killed. His mother's name was Bint Al-Saleel ibn Abdullah the brother of Abdullah ibn Jurayr Al-Bujali.

When Imam Hussain (a) was lying on the ground in Karbala nearing his last moments, Abdullah ibn Hassan ran down and hugged his uncle. Bahr ibn Ka'b swung his sword to strike Imam Hussain (a). Abdullah covered the Imam (a) and stuck his arm out to stop the blow. Bahr chopped Abdullah's arm off with that strike. Harmala ibn Kahil Al-Asadi then shot Abdullah with arrow that killed him while he was in the arms of Imam Hussain (a).

11. AOUN IBN ABDULLAH IBN JA'FAR IBN ABI TALIB

Aoun ibn Abdullah is mentioned in Al-Ziyara, Al-Irshad, Al-Tabari, Al-Asfahani, Al-Mas'oudi, and Al-Khawarizmi. His mother was Lady Zaynab bint Ali ibn Abi Talib. Al-Tabari, however, mention that he is the son of Jumana bint Al-Museeb ibn Nujba Al-Fazari.

Aoun was killed by Abdullah ibn Qutna Al-Tihani ("Qutba" according to Al-Tabari).

12. MUHAMMAD IBN ABDULLAH IBN JA'FAR IBN ABI TALIB

He is mentioned in Al-Ziyara, Al-Irshad, Al-Tabari, Al-Asfahani, Al-Mas'oudi, and Al-Khawarizmi. His mother's name was Al-Khawsa bint Hafsa ibn Thaqeef of the Bakr ibn Wael tribe. He was killed by Amer ibn Nahshal Al-Tamimi ("Al-Taymi" according to Al-Tabari).

13. JA'FAR IBN 'AQEEL IBN ABI TALIB

Ja'far ibn 'Aqeel is mentioned in Al-Ziyara, Al-Irshad, Al-Tabari, Al-Asfahani, and Al-Khawarizmi. His mother's name was Um Al-Thaghr bint Amer ibn Al-Hissan Al-Ameri, from the Kilab tribe. Al-Tabari cites to Ummul Baneen bint Al-Shaqar ibn Al-Hidhab as his mother.

Ja'far ibn 'Aqeel was killed by 'Urwa ibn Abdullah Al-Khath'ami. Al-Tabari and Al-Ziyara say that he was killed by Bishr ibn Hout Al-Hamadani.

14. ABDUL-RAHMAN IBN 'AQEEL IBN ABI TALIB

He is mentioned in Al-Ziyara, Al-Irshad, Al-Tabari, Al-Asfahani, and Al-Khawarizmi. Abdul-Rahman ibn 'Aqeel was killed by 'Uthman ibn Khalid ibn Asyad Al-Juhani and Basheer ibn Hout Al-Qayidhi. In Al-Ziyara, it says he was killd by 'Umar ibn Khalid ibn Asad Al-Juhani.

15. ABDULLAH IBN MUSLIM IBN 'AQEEL IBN ABI TALIB

Abdullah ibn Muslim is mentioned by Al-Ziyara, Al-Tabari, Al-Asfahani, Al-Mas'oudi, and Al-Khawarizmi. His mother was Ruqayya bin Ali ibn Abi Talib.

He was killed by Amr ibn Sabeeh, ("Al-Sadaa'i" according to Al-Tabari). Al-Tabari also says that Asyad ibn Malik Al-Hadrami killed Abdullah. Al-Ziyara states that he was killed Amer ibn Sa'sa'a. It also mentions that Asad ibn Malik killed him.

16. ABDULLAH IBN 'AQEEL IBN ABI TALIB

He is mentioned in Al-Ziyara, Al-Irshad, Al-Tabari, Al-Asfahani, and Al-Mas'oudi. The name that appears in Al-Ziyara Abu Abdullah ibn Muslim ibn 'Aqeel. We believe, however, that Al-Ziyara's rendition of the name is incorrect because it is the only one amongst the sources that recalls such a name. At the same time, Al-Ziyara is in agreement with Al-Tabari with the regards to his killer being Amr ibn Sabeeh Al-Saydawi or Al-Sadaa'i. In a narration by Al-Asfahani, he was killed by 'Uthman ibn Khalid ibn Asad Al-Juhan and another soldier from the tribe of Hamadan.

17. MUHAMMAD IBN SAEED IBN 'AQEEL IBN ABI TALIB.

He is mentioned in Al-Ziyara, Al-Irshad, Al-Tabari, and Al-Isfahani. Muhammad ibn Saeed was killed by Laqeet ibn Yasir

Al-Juhani ("Laqeet ibn Nashir Al-Juhani" according to Al-Ziyara).

* * *

The seventeen names above are the names that we have verified as the Hashimite martyrs of Karbala. The primary sources have all mentioned these particular names. The names that have not been mentioned in the overwhelming majority of the primary sources will be listed below, though we are uncertain that they were martyred in Karbala. We postulate that these individuals were actually martyred in different places after the battle of Karbala, and the narrators and historians mixed between them. Still, there is a possibility that our conclusion that the total number of Hashimite martyrs were seventeen, particularly limited to the seventeen above, could be wrong. The number could be greater than the number we have come to, and could include names we have not mentioned above. Thus, the list below goes to encompass such a possibility.

1. ABU BAKR IBN ALI IBN ABI TALIB

He is mentioned in Al-Irshad, Al-Khawarizmi, and Al-Asfahani. His martyrdom is mentioned as "uncertain" in Al-Tabari. Al-Asfahani stated that his name was not known. In Al-Khawarizmi, he is referred to as Abdullah.

His mother's name was Layla bint Mas'oud ibn Khalid ibn Malik Al-Thaqafi. Al-Asfahani said that he was killed by a man from the Hamadan tribe. It is also said that he was found dead in a ditch and no one knew who killed him. This statement from Al-Asfahani pushes us further to doubt his martyrdom in Karbala.

2. UBAYDALLAH IBN ABDULLAH IBN JA'FAR IBN ABI TALIB

Ubaydallah is mentioned by Al-Asfahani and Al-Khawarizmi. His mother's name was Al-Kharsa bint Hafsa. Al-Asfahani said, "Ahmad ibn Sa'eed relates from Yahya ibn Al-Hassan Al-'Alawi who stated regarding Ubaydallah, 'He was killed with Hussain in the land of Karbala, may God be pleased and send his peace and blessing upon Hussain and his family.'" Ubaydallah is not discussed by anyone other than Al-Asfahani. For that we find it unlikely that he was amongst the Hashimite martyrs of Karbala.

3. MUHAMMAD IBN MUSLIM IBN 'AQEEL IBN ABI TALIB

He is mentioned by Al-Asfahani and Al-Khawarizmi, but nowhere else. He was killed by Abu Marham Al-Azdi and Laqeet ibn Ayyas Al-Juhani.

4. ABDULLAH IBN ALI IBN ABI TALIB

Shaykh Al-Mufid's Al-Irshad is the only source to mention him. Shaykh Al-Mufid states that his mother, and the mother of Abu Bakr ibn Ali mentioned above, was Layla bint Mas'oud Al-Thaqafiya. Thus, this Abdullah is different that the Abdullah ibn Ali ibn Abi Talib, whose mother is Ummul Baneen bin Huzam. The son of Ummul Baneen has been established by the primary sources as being a martyr of Karbala and is mentioned in the first seventeen names.

5. 'UMAR IBN ALI IBN ABI TALIB

He is mentioned by Al-Khawarizmi amongst those who went into the battlefield and fought.[8] Al-Khawarizmi says that his mother was Layla bint Mas'oud ibn Khalid. Thus, 'Umar would also be the brother of Abu Bakr ibn Ali mentioned above. 'Umar here is also included amongst a list of twenty-five names cited by a narration in Maqtal Al-Hussain.[9]

6. A YOUNG MAN

In his chronological list of who went out into the battlefield to fight, Al-Khawarizmi mentions him as the last martyr from the Hashimites.[10] It is also mentioned that the name of this young man is Muhammad ibn Abi Sa'eed ibn 'Aqeel. He was killed by Hani ibn Ba'eeth or Hani ibn Thabeet Al-Hadrami.

7. IBRAHIM IBN ALI IBN ABI TALIB

He is mentioned by Al-Khawarizmi.[11]

8. 'UMAR IBN HASSAN IBN ALI IBN ABI TALIB

He is mentioned by Al-Khawarizmi.[12]

9. MUHAMMAD IBN 'AQEEL IBN ABI TALIB

He is mentioned by Al-Khawarizmi.[13]

10. JA'FAR IBN MUHAMMAD IBN 'AQEEL IBN ABI TALIB

He is mentioned by Al-Khawarizmi.[14]

BURIAL SITES

THE BODIES DURING THE BATTLE

It seems that from some of the texts, Al-Tabari and Shaykh Al-Mufid, that Imam Hussain (a) set up a tent designated for the bodies of the martyrs. It is for certain that the bodies of the Hashimites were carried to a designated place, most probably this tent. We are not certain, however, about the bodies of the non-Hashimites. If they were placed in the same tent, in another place, or if they remained in the battlefield – we cannot say for sure. Still, we elect that the higher probability is that all the bodies, including the non-Hashimites, were carried off of the battlefield per custom and tradition. The style of fighting, after the first offensive, was that of a duel setup. One fighter from the camp of Imam Hussain (a) would come forward and then be challenged by a soldier from the Umayyad camp. Whenever a duel would end, there would be a break in time on the battlefield for either camp to carry off their fallen warrior. This was especially plausible given the limited size of Imam

Hussain's (a) camp. They were so few that it would not have taken much time to pause and carry off the bodies of the martyred fighters.

Therefore, it is more probable that the bodies were carried off the battlefield but then placed in a different tent or designated spot than the Hashimite martyrs. Perhaps Imam Hussain (a) willed it – given his knowledge of the outcome of the battle and that the warriors' heads would be severed and placed on spears – to preserve the identities of the bodies. Another consideration that supports our inference is the presence of the Hashimites' families. Every Hashimite martyr in Karbala had a mother, wife, daughter, aunt or sister present amongst the women. To have a special tent for the Hashimite martyrs was Imam Hussain's (a) sensitivity and consideration to the situation's emotional and familial dimensions. To allow the women to mourn their fathers, sons, brothers, husbands, and nephews was extremely important. They would be able to see their bodies, embrace them, cry over them, and grieve together for whatever little hours remained. This was a massacre – a tragedy like no other. Imam Hussain (a) was well aware of the weight of it on the women and did what he could to lessen the burden.

The texts we mentioned above say that when Ali Al-Akbar was martyred, "…Hussain came forward to his son with his other children. He said, 'Carry your brother.' They carried him from where he was killed and placed him in front of the tent…"[1]

They also describe what happened when Al-Qasim, the son of Imam Hassan (a), was killed. The narrator, Hamid ibn Muslim says,

> ...*Hussain carried him off, and it was as if I saw the feet of the young man dragging on the ground. Hussain held him with his chest touching his. I asked myself, 'What is he doing?' He carried him and placed his body next to his son Ali and the other fallen soldiers from his family...* [2]

Shaykh Al-Mufid relates two similar narrations to what Al-Tabari provides.[3] The Shaykh also provides another narration, regarding the burial of the martyrs, that supports our inference on the bodies. "... And they, Banu Asad, dug graves by the feet of Hussain (a) for the Hashimite and non-Hashimite martyrs, who were killed around him, and gathered and buried all together."[4] The word "gathered" here infers that the Hashimites and non-Hashimites were in separate places. However, the secription of the martyrs being "around him" in the excerpt may lead the reader to think that the bodies of the non-Hashimites were dispersed and not gathered in one place, or that they were gathered in a number of locations. This opinion is very weak due to the reasons we have just mentioned. We will see that Al-Mufeed's words are unsettled in this regard.

The Burial of the Martyrs and their Graves

Al-Mas'oudi said, "… The people of Amer, the tribe of Asad, buried Hussain and his companions a day after they were killed."[5] This would mean that the burial took place on the afternoon of the 11ᵗʰ of Muharram. Shaykh Al-Mufid, however, indicates that Banu Asad buried the martyrs after Umar ibn Saad left Karbala. Umar ibn Saad left after sunset on the 11ᵗʰ of Muharram.

Shaykh Al-Mufid said,

> *And when Ibn Saad left, people from Banu Asad staying at Al-Ghadhiriya[6] came down to Hussain (a) and his fallen companions. They prayed on their bodies and buried Hussain (a) where his grave is currently located. Then they buried his son Ali ibn Hussain Al-Asghar at his feet. They dug graves for the martyrs of his family and companions – that were killed around him – gathered them and buried them all together by the feet of Hussain (a). They then buried Al-Abbas ibn Ali, peace be upon them both, in the place he was killed, which is on the path to Al-Ghadhiriya where he is buried now.[7]*

In another place Shaykh Al-Mufid said,

> *… And they – the Hashimite martyrs – are all buried by the feet of Hussain (a) in his shrine. A grave was dug for them and their bodies were all placed in that grave to-*

gether, except Al-Abbas ibn Ali (a). He was buried at the place he was killed, on the banks of the river on the path to Al-Ghadhiriya. His grave is apparent. The graves of his brothers and family members are not distinct, however. The visitor pays salutations to them at the grave of Hussain (a), he directs himself to the ground near the feet of Hussain (a), with Ali ibn Hussain (a) in his salutations as well. It is said that he is the closest one buried to Hussain (a).[8]

And of the companions of Hussain (a) – may God bless those that were killed with him – they were buried around him. We do not know their exact burial places after research and verification; however, we do not doubt that are buried within Al-Ha'ir.[9] May God be pleased with them and reward them with the vastness of Paradise.[10]

* * *

And here we have two notes.

First, the narration above contradicts the one before it. The first narration tells us that all of the martyrs, Hashimite and non-Hashimite alike, were buried in one collective grave together. The second narration seems to say that the Hashimites were buried in one grave, while the non-Hashimites were buried in various graves around Imam Hussain (a).

Second, there are two graves that we would like to bring some attention two. The first is the grave of Habib ibn Mudaher Al-Asadi. That grave is only feet away from the grave of Imam Hussain (a), and is near the direction of the Imam's (a) head. The second is the grave of Al-Hur ibn Yazid Al-Riyahi. Al-Hur's grave a few kilometers away from the shrine of Imam Hussain (a). These facts contradict both of the mentioned narrations related by Shaykh Al-Mufid. Moreover, we have not found any of the reputable historians to mention anything indisputably reliable in this respect.

Sayyid Muhsin Al-Ameen, God rest his soul, said in A'yan Al-Shia, "It is said that the tribe of Asad buried Habib ibn Mudaher by himself at the head of Hussain (a), where his grave currently is, taking special care of him because he was an Asadi. The Tamim tribe carried Al-Hur ibn Yazid Al-Riyahi about a mile away from Hussain (a), and buried him there; also taking special care of him. Al-Mufid does not mention this; however, this is what became common knowledge. The fact that people rely on this and act on it is not without justification or proof."[11]

And God knows best.

INDICATIONS

THE ELITE

The sources do not permit, except in an unsatisfying limited capacity, to directly learn about the social status and personal lives of the martyrs of Karbala. If we exclude the handful of men that we know, in great detail, were significant members in their tribes and communities, the majority of the martyrs remain unknown with regards to their social status. We know nothing of them but their names.

However we know based on some of the texts that the majority of the martyrs were not unknowns for the masses. Rather they were of caliber in their respective communities. We know they represented a specific faction that was highly respected by the people. They were met by varying degrees of admiration or enmity by those who knew them.

This is supported by the statement of Amro Ibn Al-Hajaj Al-Zubaidi[1] in which he warned Umayyad soldiers from dueling with the revolutionaries, saying,

> *Woe to you fools! Wait! Do you know who you are fighting? You are fighting 'Fursan Al-Masr' [the nights of the realms], 'Ahl Al-Basaer' [the people of insight], and a [self-sacrificing] faction.*[2]

"Fursan Al-Masr" is a term used in militant communities, which the Arab-Islamic community was at the time, referring to the special dignitaries in the community. Excelling in the military was one of the best means to attain a notable status and demanding respect in society. In fact, this quality made people give a blind eye to any defects a person possessing it might have.[3]

"Ahl Al-Basaer"[4] is a term referring to those who are judicious and make their decisions based on Islamic principles, not pecuniary considerations.

Thus, we are before a group of individuals who represent the elite, the ones conscious of Islam in the Islamic community at the time. This group derives its uniqueness and excellence from its members' positive attributes, their consciousness of Islam, and their commitment to its principled positions; contrary to the traditional tribal chieftains who derive their power from sheer tribal considerations. Nonetheless, this elite contains many members who combined both the consciousness of Islam and the loyalty of their tribes to their persons.

From what we have presented as to the elements of this elite group, it becomes clear to us that this group is the contrast to the traditional tribal elite that managed tribal politics. The tribal elite dealt with the Umayyad clan and attained official recognition of their leadership. If this tribal elite had a strong following, then the conscious elite was not without any support base, even though we think it is minor compared to the traditional base.

There is no doubt that the regime and its supporters from the traditional chiefs understood the danger of this elite because it is an elite that cannot be dealt with using traditional means. Its loyalty cannot be bought at the cost of its principles because it is from "Ahl Al-Basaer." And with what minor tribal credit it has, it is able to influence the tribal masses. The minor influence does not diminish the danger this group has because all of the efforts of change start out small. Thus, the conscious elite presents great danger. That is why the regime's major concern was to terminate the revolution – with its minor power comprised of those men – before the days allow it to pick up momentum and inspire "Ahl Al-Basaer" and their followers to express their outward support for the revolution and join it.

The traditional leaders undoubtedly understood that this elite from "Ahl Al-Basaer" would threaten their positions if they were to succeed. Consequently, they genuinely helped the regime in executing its plan of killing all of the revolutionaries, and making them an example for others.

The topic needs further examination of the Prophetic traditions and other texts to understand the history of the development of this term and its formation as part of the intellectual culture of the Muslim.

It is probable that this term derived from a former term that was used to refer to some of the companions which is "Ahl Al-Niya." It was used for Abi Al-Darda ('Uwaymer Ibn Zaid Al-Khazraji), "Abu Al-Darda was amongst the elevated compansions of the Messenger of God (s) and was known to be of 'Ahl Al-Niya' [those of pure intentions]."[5]

It is also probable that what is meant by "Ahl Al-Niya" is those with high morals and pure souls.

THE ARABS AND THE MAWALI[1]

When we study the relationship of the Mawali with Hussain's Revolution and the proofs of this relationship, we must exclude the Mawali of Hussain and Ali because their relationship is natural, deriving from the fact that their masters are its leaders. Thus, it is a specific relationship that is not indicative of the general position of the Mawali and is absolutely not appropriate to assess their position. The specific research topic is the non-Hashemite Mawali who participated in the revolution in one-way or another. The participation of those individuals can be of significance and indication if it reaches a certain level of quantity and variation.

If we look into the percentage of Mawali in the small revolutionary forces with Hussain, we will find it is a slim percentage that does not exceed ten percent of the total revolutionarie. If we exclude the Mawali of Hussain, the remaining Mawali we have from the names that reached us are six; John servant of

Abi Thar Al-Ghafari, Zaher servant of Amro Ibn Al-Hamq Al-Khuzaei, Salem servant of Bani Al-Madaniya Al-Kalbi, Salem servant of Amer Al-Abdi, Saad Ibn Abdullah servant of Amro Ibn Khaled Al-Azadi, Shawthab servant of Shaker Ibn Abdullah Al-Hamadani Al-Shakeri.

If the phenomena of the presence of the Mawali in Hussain's Revolution was limited to the participation of the few martyred in Karbala, it would not have any historical significance. However, the phenomena of the presence of the Mawali in Hussain's Revolution and their relationship with it tremendously exceed this limited scope to other areas. There are signs before and after Ashura that show a relationship of some sort, perhaps grand, between the Mawali and Hussain's Revolution. It is possible that this had significant indications of the commencement of the great and dangerous role of the Mawali in directing the movement of history in the Islamic world.

From these signs is that when Ubaidallah Ibn Ziyad wanted to spy on Muslim Ibn Aqeel, he did not use in this assignment an Arab, rather "he called a servant by the name of Ma'qal and gave him 3,000 and told him, 'Leave so that you ask about the man who the Kufans are paying allegiance to and tell him that you are a man from Homs...'"[2]

Another sign is the widow who Muslim sought to hide in her house after his movement failed and the people abandoned him, Lady Taw'a. She was a servant of Muhammad Ibn Al-Ash'ath.[3] She welcomed him into her home as soon as she knew him, without showing concern for what could inflict her for hosting him. She hid him knowing he is wanted by the regime.

Does Ubaidallah Ibn Ziyad's decision to select a spy from the Mawali instead of an Arab to spy on Muslim Ibn Aqeel indicative that the Umayyad regime recognized that the Mawali staunchly sympathized with the revolution and its men, and that there was a secret relationship between the revolution and groups of Mawali such that the revolutionaries would trust a stranger if he is a Mawla more than if he was an Arab from the Levant that they have no way to verify his identity? There is no way to disguise an Iraqi man who can easily be identified if he was asked about in his tribe. Also, is Muslim Ibn Awsaja's[4] answer to the spy without any precaution a confirmation of the Umayyad clan's accurate assessment of the relationship between the Mawali and the revolution?

Is the answer of Lady Taw'a to Muslim Ibn Aqeel and hiding him in her home, after he informed her that the Kufans have betrayed him, indicative that she acted in conformity with a positive emotional position she had towards the revolution, a feeling that overwhelmed her to not think of the dangerous implications of her actions?

We do not have conclusive answers to these questions, although we believe it is more probable that the political and social considerations during that time pushes us to favor affirmative and positive answers.

We know that the Mawali had a strong relationship with Imam Ali Ibn Abi Taleb originating from the Imam's just governance which made them equal to other Muslims. Some tribal leaders detested this relationship. Al-Ash'ath Ibn Qais told Imam Ali: "O Commander of the Faithful, these Hamra have surpassed us in their closeness to you."[5]

It is certain that these people, during the days of Yazid and Muawiya, continued to remember that their life during the few years of Imam Ali Ibn Abi Taleb's governance was more prosperous, stable, and dignified than under the governance of Muawiya Ibn Abi Sufyan. They now lived in abasement. Muawiya desired to kill half of them in some way because he feared the political implications resulting from an increase in their population and what follows of political dilemmas.[6]

Thus, it is undoubtedly natural in this situation for the Mawali to take advantage of any opportunity to improve their awful condition after Imam Ali's tenure.

If Ubaidallah Ibn Ziyad did not take the initiative to extinguish Muslim Ibn Aqeel's movement, and if it was permitted for the revolution to continue for a few more days before it was terminated, the role of the Mawali would have been unraveled to us much more clearly than what we have now. Most likely, we would have witnessed that their presence and participation in the revolution would have been much greater and more expansive than what is reflected by the remains of the revolution's recorded history.

Few Arabs leaders and dignitaries were moving towards the revolution, motivated by religious enthusiasm and the vigilance of a small minority. Additionally, they were inspired to reclaim governance from the Levant and return Kufa to its previous great status.

The Mawali were moving towards the revolution inspired to change their dreadful conditions back to the days of Imam Ali. However, there was a small minority, represented by the martyrs that flocked towards the revolution motivated by a pure understanding of Islam, and recognizing the deviant nature of the Umayyad governance.

What transpired after Hussain's Revolution in a few years revealed the depth and extent of the relationship of the Mawali. When Al-Mukhtar Ibn Abi Ubaid Al-Thaqafy[7] rose in Kufa carrying the banner of protecting the poor and avenging Hussain and his household, both the Arabs and the Mawali supported him. However, aftewards the dominant majority of the Arabs abandoned him because they refused his financial and social policies with respect to the Mawali. The Mawali remained steadfast with him until the painful end in the face of the governance of Ibn Zubair which was no less discriminating than Umayyad rule.[8]

We can say that the Mawali during the year 60 AH were in the early stages of having awareness of their poor condition compared to what Islam secured them in a respectful status equal to the status of Arabs in the Islamic nation. They were also in the early stages of having awareness of their capability if leadership was offered to them that would translate their pain and aspirations into action. Hussain's Revolution matured their sense of awareness of their reality and rights as Muslims, as well as having cultivated their awareness of their presence as a grand force in Islamic society capable of driving change.

When the uprising of Al-Mukhtar Ibn Abi Ubaid Al-Thaqafy was launched, the Arab-Islamic society witnessed the new power of Mawali. They fought viciously for noble principles – ones that the ruling government utters as slogans, but does not apply in its daily dealings with the populace. Al-Mukhtar genuinely attempted to employ the Islamic propositions of equating between Arabs and the Mawali. This was a favorable position for him. However, he failed due to the bigotry and short sightedness of tribal leaders. Thus, he was forced to rely on the Mawali and a small base of astute Arab.

This division that inflicted the pro-revolution masses in Iraq – between the Arab Muslims and the non-Arab Muslims – provided an opportunity for Ibn Al-Zubair to extinguish the revolution. However, this point was a watershed after which a deep and expansive change took hold of the Muslim nation - culminating in the Abbasid regime seizing power.

NORTHERN AND SOUTHERN ARABS

Most of the non-Hashemite revolutionaries are Southern Arabs from Yemen.

Perhaps, this could have been a sign that those that swore allegiance to Muslim Ibn Aqeel were primarily Southern Arab. It seems they represented the vast majority of the revolutionary audience.

One of the indicators is that when Ubaidallah Ibn Ziyad came to Kufa, Muslim Ibn Aqeel moved from Al-Mukhtar Ibn Abi Ubaid Al-Thaqafy's residence who is from Mudar (Northern Arab) to the home of one of the top leaders of the Southern Arabs in Kufa (Urwa Ibn Hani Al-Murady).

Another critical indicator that supports this is that when Ubaidallah Ibn Ziyad wanted to arrest Muslim Ibn Aqeel following the failure of his movement in Kufa, he chose Northern Arab soldiers, from Qais, to execute this task. No one in that battalion was from Southern Arabia – Yemen – except for the commanding general, Abd Al-Rahman Ibn Al-Ash'ath.[1]

If Muslim Ibn Aqeel's movement in Kufa had this Yemeni feature, we realize that there was a very importantly indicative matter to Imam Hussain when he announced his refusal to pay allegiance to Yazid Ibn Muawiya in Hijaz.

When Hussain determined to leave Medina to Mecca, then decided to leave Mecca to Iraq, on his way to Iraq, he received advice from various people with diverse mentalities and affiliations, to direct himself to Yemen instead of Iraq.

He received this piece of advice from his brother Muhammad Ibn Al-Hanafiya on the eve of departure from Medina to Mecca. Muhammad Ibn Al-Hanafiya told Hussain:

> … *Leaving toward Mecca. If you find a safe home there, that is our aspiration. If not, then leave to Yemen. For they are the allies of your grandfather, father, and brother. Their hearts are more merciful and kind. Their lands are most vast. Their reasoning is most judicious…*[2]

Additionally, he received similar advice from Abdullah Ibn Abbas in Mecca. Abdullah told him:

> …*If you decide that you must leave, go to Yemen. It is a vast land of forts and valleys. There are devotees of your father there, and you will be isolated from [enemies].*[3]

He received similar advice from Al-Turmah Ibn Uday Al-Taei at the Udayb Al-Hujanat. He came as a guide to four men from Kufa who had joined Hussain (a) after the martyrdom of Muslim ibn Aqeel.[4]

> *… If you want to settle in a land where God will protect you until you come to an opinion and you have a clear vision of what you will do, then walk [with me] until I take you to the fortress of our mountain which is called Ajaa… Then I will walk with you until I take you to the village. Then we will send men from Ajaa and Salma from [the tribe of] Tai. By God, you will not pass ten days until [the tribe of] Tai comes to you both infantry and horsemen.[5]*

We realize this phenomenon – Yemeni support for the revolution – continued even after the events of Karbala and the reign of Yazid Ibn Muawiya. Its implications had its effects on the aftermath.

The Kufans doffed – after the death of Yazid Ibn Muawiya – the governance of the Umayyad clan and governorship of Ibn Ziyad. They wanted to appoint a governor until they figured out what they wanted to do.

> *A group said that Omar Ibn Saad Ibn Abi Waqas is fit for it. When they prepared to assign him governor, a group of women from Hamdan and others from Kahlan, Al-Ansar, Rabi'a, and Al-Nakha' entered the mosque and started crying and whaling. They mourned Hussain and charged that Omar Ibn Saad was not satisfied with*

merely killing Hussain, but now wishes to rule over
Kufa. The people started crying and turned their back
against Omar. The women of Hamdan took the lead in
this effort.[6]

* * *

This phenomenon of Yemeni support of Hussain's Revolution
pushes us to realize the the significance of the discrepancy in
the ratio of Southern Arab revolutionaries as compared to their
Northern Arab comrades in the revolting forces in Karbala.
Although this was a very limited discrepancy in term of number, it is nonetheless a significant indication of the quality of
the revolution in terms of standards and principles. Muawiya
had discovered that Mudar is not aligned with him and had
become dependent in stabilizing his rule on the Yemeni factor.
Such was the case with his son Yazid, whose mother is a Yemeni from the tribe of Kalb. Despite all this, we find the percentage of Southern Arab men is greater than the percentage of
Northern Arabs in the ranks of the revolutionary forces.

Revolution is a political operation. It would have been natural
for it to be based on the political conventions of the time – that
is, for the audience of this revolution to be recruited by utiliza-
tion of the common discourse on tribal rivalry. However, what
transpired was contrary to this apparent conclusion. The revolutionary base formed slowly as a result of people's awareness of
Islamic principles. The revolution engaged with its audience

through their personal beliefs and not through their tribal interests.

Does that mean that the Northern Arabs were distant from the revolution? It is certain that this conclusion is completely invalid. Moreover, it is certain that the Northern Arab were a vital and significant faction in the revolution, although we cannot find a 'Mudari' or 'Adnani' phenomenon. We do notice that some of the texts refer to the prominent role of the Northern Arabs – from the Qais bloodline – in supporting the government to eradicate the revolution.

We mention in this respect what we discussed earlier; that the force that captured Muslim Ibn Aqeel was from Qais.[7] There is a significant poetic text that brings to light the tribal situation. It demonstrates that Qais is the greatest enemy responsible for killing Hussain. Sulayman ibn Qita Al-Muhariby Al-Tabei[8] recited some versus of poetry mourning Hussain:

> *And the Martyr of [Karbala] from the Hashimite clan*
> *Humbled the necks of Muslims, and so they were humbled*
> *With Ghani lies a drop of our blood*
> *We will have retribution for it someday in the place where it reached*
> *If Qays were to be impoverished, we would mend their poverty*
> *And Qays would kill us if the foot slips.[9]*

The poet in mourning Hussain mentions Qais (Qais Aylan Ibn Mudar) and remembers Ghani (from Ghatfan, from Qais Aylan) and holds them responsible for killing Hussain, threatening revenge.

* * *

The revolutionaries of Karbala comprised a small base, in its two wings of Southern and Northern Arabs. However, it represented the elite. We must realize that many of the revolutionaries did not represent – in terms of quantity – their persons or families, but behind all of that, they represented large groups of tribes.

Because the revolutionaries represented the elite, they would have been capable of controlling the situation if the revolution was to succeed and they obtain governance. They were capable in the case that the revolution did not succeed – as was the reality – of erupting a volcano of anger in the hearts of a massive amount people against the deviant government, and to put them on the path of true vigilance. Furthermore, they were capable of creating a base that continuously fed the revolutions that were to come. That is what occurred in reality.

We postulate that the Umayyad regime's personnel had discovered this truth and decided to confront it.

This would certainly explain why they employed such methods to confront the revolution and crush it with brutality, even though there was no military or security need for such measures.

They followed an atypical and abnormal method in murdering a number of revolutionaries in Kufa.

They beheaded Muslim Ibn Aqeel and launched his body from the top of the palace to the ground, crushing every bone in his body. They beheaded Hani Ibn Urwa in the market after he was capruted and tied. They were both dragged by their feet in the markets of Kufa.[10]

They launched Abdullah Ibn Baqtur from the top of the palace, crushing every bone in his body. He had some life remaining in him and so they slaughtered him.[11]

Ubaidallah Ibn Ziyad ordered to throw Qais Ibn Mishir Al-Saidawi from the top of the palace. His body severed into pieces and he died.[12]

After that, they employed the method of brutal eradication which did not leave a single individual living from the small group of revolutionaries in Karbala. Although their numbers were minute, a large force was organized[13] and all of Iraq was put under state of emergency. Iraq was governed by marshal law. The regime wanted to avoid falling into any errors that would allow for one of the top leaders to escape its hold.

The measures to eradicate and destroy the revolution consisted of extreme methods despite the fact that military force was not required in the first place. The revolutionaries were besieged, disconnected from any sources for supplies. They were tortured through thirst –kids, women, and animals included. Then they were killed and trampled by horses. Next, the heads of the prominent Islamic figures were severed and the women were held captive, especially the Hashemites.

Why all of this unnecessary cruelty?

The regime wanted to make an example out of all of the revolutionaries. It desired to destroy the psyche of the unconformist members of the tribes. The state wished to crush the psychological fortitude of the revolutionary factions in Arab society – the Northern Arabs as well as the Yemen Arab whose revolution was distressing to the state, as they were the close allies of the government and ruling class.

The revolutionaries did not act with a tribal spirit or mentality. They acted in accordance with their Islamic creed and thus escaped the restrains that the government imposed on them. It is possible that the regime did not intend to act with such cruelty – that is if we believe some of the narrations stating that Ibn Ziyad accepted, for some time, to end the siege, and permit Hussain and his companions to disperse in the lands, while the issue goes back to the counsel of the Muslims (a form of Shura) – however, we doubt the credibility of these narrations.

The regime treated the revolutionaries with such extreme cruelty that would remain as an example for people to talk about. It discovered that the revolution easily attracted certain leaders who were supposed to be loyal to its camp – Zuhayr Ibn Al-Qain Al-Bajli and others – because these individuals are from the social elite; notables and tribal chiefs. The traditional tribal chieftains felt that if this trend was allowed to continue, it would overtake their authority over their clans and tribes. Thus, they became complicit in the government's actions with full faith and enthusiasm. They wished to protect their interests in preserving power and influence.

The method the government adopted with the revolutionaries was not due to any need for military intervention. Rather, it was a political operation meant to make an example out of the revolutionaries. At the same time, it fulfilled the desire to take revenge and perpetuate hatred.

HASHEMITES, TALIBIDS, AND ABBASIDS

There is no doubt that the Hashemites were behind the revolution. But which of the Hashemites initiated it?

The revolution was fueled by Hashemites from Talibid[1] line – including Ali Ibn Abi Talib, Jaafer Ibn Abi Talib, and Aqeel Ibn Abi Talib. As to the Abbasids – the sons of Abbas Ibn Abd Al-Mutalib – none of them participated or were mentioned in the events, from start to finish, with the exception of Abdullah Ibn Abbas when he advised Hussain to not travel to Iraq, and then his conversation with Abdullah Ibn Al-Zubair after the departure of Hussain. The conversation may give the impression that Abdullah Ibn Abbas was upset. But this was not because Hussain left to a tragic destination. Rather, it was due to the fact that Hussain was the center of attention in Mecca and, in his absence, it bcame the exclusive domain of Abdullah Ibn Al-Zubair. [2]

After the conclusion of the revolution, there was no significant mentioning of any of the Abbasids commenting on the events of Karbala and condemning it.

Following the revolution, there were a number of powerful revolutions in Iraq, Hijaz, and Iran led by Hashemites, all of which were Talibids and none Abbasids.

The Abbasids were enjoying the Caliphs' gifts and luxurious life while the Talibids were burning in the fire of revolutions.

Although the Talibids and others led many bloody revolutions, they did not succeed in taking over the governance from the Umayyad clan. The Abbasids succeeded in that.

Why?

It seems that the Abbasids decided to work for their interests at a very early stage. Their relationship with the Alids was very superficial and interest-driven.[3] Thus, from the advent of Imam Hussain's (a) revolution, they persistently refused to contribute any effort that would serve the rise of the Alid line to governance. They benefited from their popularity since they were Hashemites oppressed by the government. At the same time, they benefitted from the government since they were Hashemites that did not participate with their cousins in the revolution, sparing their power to promote their personal interests.

The Abbasids finally succeeded in seizing governance, taking advantage of two factors.

First: As we mentioned, they took advantage of the influence they had with the masses which came as a result of all the revolutions that the Talibids and others initiated. When they proceeded to propagate for themselves, their propagators did not specify who exactly they are propagating for. The propagation was to seek approval from the Household of Muhammad (s). The people understood from this that the person who is promoted is an Alid, due to the resounding presence that the Alids had in public awareness. Only the propagators and the elite knew that the propagation was for the Abbasid line. When the time was right, they announced that they were referring to the authority allegedly conferred by Abi Hashem Ibn Muhammad Ibn Al-Hanafiyya, Imam Ali's grandson, to Ali Ibn Abdullah Ibn Abbas.[4]

Second: The Abbasids permitted for themselves to cooperate with the parties that the Alids did not permit themselves to deal with – namely, the deviant groups in Islam and the Iranian groups that are doubted with respect to their Islam. The Alids generally cooperated with Arab and Iranian parties whose Islam was genuine and whose positions were firm, principled, and clear against the parties that had a dubious Muslim character. This led these parties to seek other allies, which they found in the Abbasids.

Here, it becomes clear to us why the Imams of Progeny (a), starting with Imam Zein Al-Abideen, had a negative position towards the revolutions established by the Hassanids and Hussainids.

It also becomes apparent why Imam Abu Abdullah Jaafer Al-Sadiq (a) refused the offer of Abi Salma Al-Khalal, one of the major Abbasid propagators,[5] to take governance after the propagation matured against the Umayyad clan and Abu Muslim Al-Khorasani had announced his revolution in Khorasan.[6]

The Imams of Ahlulbayt clearly understood that the forces the Alids relied on were fatigued, unable to lead a successful revolutionary movement in a large geographical area. Thus, a revolution that is dependent on such forces is inevitably destined to fail. The results would only be to incur the wrath of the Umayyads against the entire nation.

Conversely, they recognized that the qualified forces able to lead a successful revolution are mostly non-Islamic. Thus, they did not permit themselves to deal with these forces. Still, they did not stand against the Abbasid led movement, as the toppling of the Umayyad regime was a historical and civilizational request that could not be opposed. They also knew that Islam will merge all groups that were suspect in their creed into the Islamic community, religiously and civically.

The Imams of Ahlulbayt remained committed to this position during the Abbasid era. They instructed their followers to not participate in this type of activity. Moreover, they advised their cousins from the Alids to avoid initiating revolutions destined to fail, although they were not able to affect them.

THE YOUTH AND ELDERS

Some of the texts indicate that this person or that from the martyrs of Hussain's Revolution were from the youth – such as Ubaidallah and Abdullah, the sons of Yazid, and others similar to them. Likewise, some of the texts indicate that certain martyrs were elders, such as the companions and their contemporaries including Muslim Ibn Awsaja, Anas Ibn Al-Harith Al-Kahili, and others. However, at this stage in our research, we cannot obtain a complete and detailed insight into every revolutionary's age when he committed to the revolution.

We face this difficulty particularly with the large revolutionary base that paid allegiance to Muslim Ibn Aqeel in Kufa. What is the ratio of elders to youth?

Abi Makhnaf's text which explains how the people abandoned Muslim Ibn Aqeel when he started his movement in Kufa after the arrest of Hani Ibn Irwa states:

> *The women would come to her son or brother and tell him, 'Leave and others will suffice in your stead.' The*

> *man would come to his son or brother and tell him, 'To-*
> *morrow the people of the Levant would come after you,*
> *what good would you do with war and violence...?[l]*

This text portraying the defeatist stance with respect to Muslim Ibn Aqeel's movement reveals to the contemplating researcher that a high percentage of the fighters that rose with Muslim Ibn Aqeel were from the youth. They were the sons and brothers and not the fathers and husbands.

We admit that this proof is not conclusive, but it pushes us to lean towards what is the natural norm, which is that the will for change is usually found in the youth and not the elders that typically tend to be conservative and prefer to hold on to the status quo. However, in this case – Hussain's Revolution – we face an exceptional situation. It is very probable that there was a high percentage of elders, specifically in Kufa, that answered the call of the revolution. These people experienced first hand Imam Ali's political, social, and financial policies and also experienced after him Muawiya's political, social, and financial policies. They witnessed the drastic differences between the two. With direct exposure to these two methods of governance, they understood Muawiya's violation of Islamic principles and teachings. Due to this experience and knowledge, they were qualified to understand Imam Hussain's revolution and respond to it more than the younger generation which did not know but Muawiya's ways. The younger generation suffered only one dimension of the experience which was Muawiya's policies pertaining to them and their country. They only heard teales about the other dimension. Additionally, they were less aware about the principles of Islam and less attached to them than their fathers.

But shouldn't the natural tendency of the elders to favor stability override their awareness of the necessity of change due to their experience with Ali and Muawiya?

And how could we say that these elders are more aware of the Islamic principles than the younger generation?

Most of the elders were nomads that were raised in the desert. The conquests brought them to the new lands where they were taught by companions that accompanied the invading armies. In the year 60 AH, most of the older generation was lacking in its understanding of Islam, its values, and great manners – that is, if we exclude knowledge of worship rituals. As to the younger generation, it was raised in these lands in Muslim homes. It received the Islamic teachings through Friday sermons and teaching circles in Mosques. Furthermore, the younger generation received these teachings with innocent intellects and souls free from the sediments of the age of ignorance – except that which they inherited from the older generation. Undoubtedly, their Islamic faith is better than that of their fathers. Thus, they were more capable of understanding the Islamic justifications for Hussain's Revolution, dissent, and make decisions. Consequently, they were more qualified to become the base of the revolution.

We think it is more probable that the majority of the revolutionaries were from the younger generation. The issue needs further examination and study based on the primary and secondary texts, if such sources can be found.

Kufa, Basra, and Hijaz

We do not have statistics that indicate, with certainty, the distribution of where the revolutionaries came from with respect to the three provinces of Kufa, Basra, and Hijaz. The narrations by the historians did not include the places of origin, except for a handful of revolutionaries. Nonetheless, we believe that the majority of the revolutionaries were Kufans. The rest were from Hijaz and Basra. Kufa was the springboard of revolution in the Islamic world. After the death of Muawiya, the idea of changing the regime was widely discussed in Kufa. Meetings were organized to plan for this change. From Kufa, the messengers proceeded to Hussain carrying the letters requesting him to lead the new movement. Those that paid allegiance to Muslim were Kufans. All of these considerations invite us to believe that the majority of the revolutionaries were from Kufa.

Kufa always stood out as the most revolutionary-driven land. Conversely, Basra was dominated by a sense of reservation and caution and Hijaz was more concerned with their luxury and security.

Thus, we believe that most of the individuals of Hijazi origin participating in the revolution – other than the Hashemites – were the servants of the Bani Hashim.

Hussain left Hijaz in revolt against a regime that everyone knew the necessity of revolting against. Even with that, no one came out to support him. His departure did not stir any enthuisiasm or drive in the people of Hijaz.

Hussain directed the call for the revolution to the dignitaries and chiefs in Basra (the heads of the five major tribes). Whoever read the letter from the dignitaries concealed it – except for Al-Munthir Ibn Al-Jaroud, who allegedly feared that the messenger was a secret agent for Ubaidallah. He took the messenger on the eve of the morning he wanted to leave to Kufa and had him read the letter. The messenger was killed.[1]

This was the position of the leaders in Basra towards the revolution. These positions seemed to be expected to a great extent from men that did not want to compromise their positions in the government and society. In fact it is incredibly surprising to see the stance of the Shia in Basra as it appears in the following text narrated by Al-Tabari on the behalf of Abi Al-Makhariq Al-Rasibi.

A group of Shia form Basra met for days in the house of a women from Abd Al-Qais knows as Maria Ibnat Saad

(or Munqith). She was a Shia. Her house was a sanctu-
ary for them to meet and discuss. When Ibn Ziyad was
informed about the coming of Hussain, he wrote to his
worker in Basra instructing him to place outposts and
keep an eye out. He said: Yazid Ibn Nabeet, who is from
Abd Al-Qais, decided to go out and support Hussain. He
had ten sons who he asked, 'Who will come out with me?'
He chose two sons to join him, Ubaidallah and Abdullah.
He said to his companions in the house of that lady, 'I
have decided to go out, and so I shall.' They responded,
'we fear for you the companions of Ibn Ziyad...'[2]

We will mention another example of the stance of the Shia
leaders of Basra in another section.

Why were the people of Basra cautious and the people of Hijaz
indifferent while the Kufans were clearly motivated?

Is the answer that Hijaz, which is no longer the center for the
Islamic Caliphate, was no longer concerned with the activities
related to the Caliphate, which inevitably will be in the Levant
or Iraq? This is in addition to Muawiya's policies which caused
the elite of Hijaz – from Quraish and others – to become con-
sumed in a life of luxury and play such that they eschewed from
any activities that might compromise this lifestyle.

The Basrans – who were always in conflict with the Kufan
tribes over who has the right to the tax collection in this or that
land[3] – were not motivated to participate in a revolution that, if

successful, would strengthen the status of Kufa, but if unsuccessful would destroy both cities.

If the answer is not due to the difference in the political and economic concerns of the two provinces, can we find an answer in the cultural climate?

Did the cultural climate of the Kufans make them more aware and alert of the deviations of their rulers, and more willing to change than the more conservative people of Hijaz and Basra.

It seems that Muawiya Ibn Abu Sufyan did realize this truth and understood this revolutionary spirit, but he sensed it in the entirety of Iraq and not only in Kufa. Thus, he instructed his son Yazid in his will,

> *Observe the people of Iraq. If they request from you to change an agent every day, then do so. Expelling an employee is more desirable for me than for 100,000 swords to be brandished against you.*[4]

Is the reference to Iraq in Muawiya's will intended chiefly for Kufa? We believe that is more probable.[5]

If the answer is not in the cultural affiliation, is it in the recent history – where the Basrans held on to the bloody images of the Battle of the Camel; when the Kufans, led by Imam Ali (a) crushed the Basran insurgency against the Imam, led by Talha, Al-Zubair, and the Mother of Believers Aisha?

Finally, is the answer in the tribal affiliations of the residents in both provinces?

We know that most of the residents in Basra were from Rabia and Mudar – Northern Arabs – while most of the residents in Kufa were from the Yemeni tribes – Southern Arab.[6] We saw in a previous section that the Southern Arabs were the majority of the revolutionaries in Karbala.

We believe it is more probable that all of these factors played a part in formulating the position of the Basrans with respect to the revolution.

The leaders of Basra were undoubtedly thinking about their positions in government and society. The Basrans were always in conflict with Kufans regarding the right to conquer this land or that. They thought any success for the revolution will be a success for Kufa, which will ultimately become the base of the nation. The Kufans were more aware of the necessity for change as a result of the culture they were raised in during Imam Ali's governance. They felt guilty for abandoning Imam Ali's government and his political thought. This dereliction of duty led Muawiya to triumph and exact vengance against Kufa. We note here that the plentiful participation of the Southern Arabs in the revolution is due to their higher level of awareness – since they were in Kufa, they were more connected with the Imam and influenced by his thoughts and teachings. Their stance was not due to tribal elements. The tribal audience base in Basra had participated in the Battle of the Camel against Imam Ali and continuously remembers their murdered soldiers. They respond to the feelings aroused by this remembrance.

THE DEGREE OF THE REVOLUTIONARY STATE

During the year 60 AH, there was a revolutionary state in the Islamic society in Iraq, Hijaz, and Iran. There is no doubt about that. There was tremendous discontent with the situation and a desire for change.

The events and situations which reflected this revolutionary state were plenty. They were most apparent in Iraq and Hijaz. In Mecca, Medina, and Kufa, the official administration was powerless in controlling the notables in society. The people discussed the necessity for reform with no reservations. Additionally, there was a massive and prompt response to Muslim Ibn Aqeel when he arrived to Kufa. Furthermore, the regime was forced to take extreme measures of caution, vigilance, and precaution. All of that is indicative of the presence of a revolutionary state.

However, this revolutionary spirit was in a paralyzed psychological state. It seems to be an intellectual state of awareness of the hopeless reality and the necessity of change. This did not reach a mobilizing emotional state.

Ubaidallah Ibn Ziyad's ability to control the situation in Kufa proves the presence of the paralyzed psyche in the city. Ibn Ziyad was able to do this with baffling ease. Before his arrival in Kufa, it was the center for revolutionary movements. Also corroborating this is the abrupt nature of how the Kufans abandoned Muslim Ibn Aqeel after he initiated his movement against Ubaidallah and after the arrest of Hani Ibn Urwa. In just a matter of hours, the revolutionaries who paid allegiance to Muslim abandoned their leader and their moral and religious obligation. Some of them joined the regime and announced their allegiance to it, while others decided to become neutral.

It seems that the spirit of the revolution did not permeate through all of Kufa. In countless families, the position of individuals varied. This is supported by the text of Abi Makhnaf where he portrays how the people parted away from Muslim Ibn Aqeel after the notables announced, from the balconies of the Royal Palace, the threats of the Umayyad regime.

> *The women would come to her son or brother and tell him, 'Leave and others will suffice in your stead.' The man would come to his son or brother and tell him, 'Tomorrow the people of the Levant would come after you...'*[1]

There was a spirit of complacency – "Leave and others will suffice in your stead" – and revolutionaries' acquiesced to it. There was a spirit of fear – "tomorrow the people of the Levant will come after you" – and the revolutionaries acquiesced to it as well. These do not reflect a healthy revolutionary state. The confinements of reality, desire to live a complacent and relaxed life, and preserving a rich livelihood; all of this would derail the revolutionary spirit and prevent it from fulfilling its role. The spirits of fear and complacency found proper psychological grounds, and thus made their impact in an exceptionally short amount of time.

Some of the proofs for the paralyzed psyche in Basra is portrayed in the following text by Isa Ibn Yazid Al-Kinani. He said:

> *When the letter from Yazid arrived to Ubaidallah Ibn Ziyad (pertaining to his governorship of Kufa), he selected five hundred individuals [to ride with him to Kufa], including Abdullah Ibn Al-Harith Ibn Nawfal and Shareek Ibn Al-A'war – a follower of Ali. It is narrated that the first [to fall behind] was Shareek. It would be said [that he fell behind with a group of people]. Then Abdullah Ibn Harith [fell behind with another group]. They hoped that Ubaidallah would [wait for them to catch up] and Hussain would precede him to Kufa.[2]*

Those that demonstrated their inability to continue the strenuous journey – and had hoped that Ubaidallah Ibn Ziyad is delayed by them, allowing Hussain to precede him to Kufa and settle there – were doubtlessly afflicted with this psychological paralysis. They hoped that Ubaidallah would not be able to take advantage of the power vacuum left by the absence of the commander in chief of the revolutionary forces. They desired change and abhorred their present circumstances. Yet, they did not want to seek change with their hands, but rather sought change through the efforts of others. If not, then why this crooked method in cheating to delay Ubaidallah Ibn Ziyad from continuing his strenuous journey to Kufa? They were, as leaders of Basra, capable of halting Ubaidallah for days simply by inciting a simple disturbance. In fact, they were able to kill him if their revolutionary spirits were healthy.

However, as we mentioned, they were suffering from a paralyzed psyche that disrupted the operation of their revolution.

Some of the indicators of this paralyzed psyche – one that drives individuals to be cunning when faced by events and precludes him from being determined and decisive in accomplishing his duties – is the attempt of the great Basran Shia leader Shareek Ibn Al-A'war to persuade Muslim Ibn Aqeel to assassinate Ubaidallah Ibn Ziyad when Shareek recovers from his illness, promising Muslim, "if my pain ends these days, I will head to Basra and will take care of things."[3] As if the success of revolutions had to wait on the recovery of its leaders from their illnesses. Muslim, in his moral position, was the chief leader. Shareek was able to delegate this assignment to any other man.

Some of the indicators of this paralyzed psyche in Hijaz and other places are the numerous suggestions that Hussain received to not go out. Even though they all recognized the legitimacy of his mission, they prohibited him from facing the Umayyads. They advised him to leave to another place other than the center of revolutions in Iraq.

We add here to the sugestions that we mentioned in previous sections the advice that Abdullah Ibn Mutee' Al-Adawi offered Imam Hussain to not confront the Umayyads.

> *I remind you of God, O son of the Messenger of God and sanctity of Islam, to not be violated. I call upon you by God to heed the sanctity of the Messenger of God (s). I call upon you by God to heed the sanctity of the Arabs. By God, if you request what is in the hands of the Umayyads, they will surely kill you. Surely if they kill you, they will never fear anyone after you. By God, it is the sanctity of Islam that will be violated, amd the sanctity of Quraish and the Arabs. So do not take this course of action. Do not go to Kufa, and do not confront the Umayyads.[4]*

This rhetoric – fueled by strain, tension, and fear – reveals conviction in the mission overtaken by fear of the consequences of committing to and working for it. It seems that Abdullah Ibn Mutee' had met Hussain before this when he left Medina. He suggested to him,

Hold on to the Grand Mosque[5] for you are the master of the Arabs. By God, the people of Hijaz do not equate anyone to you. The people flock to you from every part. Do not depart the Grand Mosque, may my uncles be sacrificed for you. By God, if you are slaughtered, we will be inslaved after you."[6]

* * *

The revolutionary spirit was present. However, it was diminished due to the paralyzed psyche that was prevalent in the people who desired change but were aware of the hopeless reality. Thus, the revolutionary state was in need of a great and violent initiator that will transform it from being just a theoretical aspiration to a high level of tension, and will make it a state of feeling able to move the person to work for changing his reality via struggle, not through mere aspirations and awaiting the actions of others. This transformation did occur in Hussain's Revolution. The reluctant and paralyzed masses turned into revolutionary audiences – in every meaning of the word. It pushed many to commit suicidal acts such as what happened to the Tawabeen during the battle of Ayn Al-Warda.[7]

The discussion between Ayoub Ibn Mishrah Al-Khaywani with Abi Al-Wadak demonstrates to us the deep and painful regret that was in the hearts and souls of the Shia classes after the Karbala Revolution.[8]

Also, the new revolutionary spirit reached a level of tension such that it placed anyone who participated in Karbala outside of society and the protection of the norms and laws. It was always inspiring and motivating for leading revolutions.

THE POLITICAL SIGNIFICANCE OF SEVERING HEADS

Severing the head of a corpse, whether the person was murdered or died of natural causes, has the same result.

What is constant in Islamic teachings is the prohibition on mutilating the body of a Muslim. We do not know of anything contrary to that at all.

In fact, what is also constant is the prohibition of mutilating the body of a non-believer, which is established via the traditions of the Messenger of God (s). With all of the wars that he engaged in with the polytheists, he never permitted or accepted anything of that sort. It was also not known of any of the caliphs succeeding him that something like that occurred during their tenure, although they were involved in many wars against the Persians and Romans. The only exception is during the era of Abu Bakr when Khalid Ibn Al-Waleed invaded the tribe of Malek Ibn Nuwaira, alleging that they were apostates. He killed them and then severed their heads[1] - actions that drew a wide array of condemnations by Muslims of the time.

With respect to Imam Ali Ibn Abi Talib, there was never an incident during all of his wars where a severed head was brought to him, where he commanded for the severing of a head, or where there was any indication of approval for such a practice.

Indeed, when Imam Ali defeated the Kharijites in Harura, he did order to sever the hand of Al-Makhdaj (Nafe' Al-Makhdaj). He said, "His mark is that his hand is like an udder. It has hairs like the whiskers of a cat. Bring me his severed hand." They brought it to him and he showcased it.[2]

This incident is one of the indicators of Prophethood. The Prophet (s) had foretold of the Kharijites and that, "their mark is a man with one of his hands – or he said his breasts – like the breast of a woman." This tradition was narrated regarding them and amongst the narrators is Al-Bukhari in his book.[3] It seems that Imam Ali ordered his hand to be showcased in order to reveal the truthfulness of the Prophet's (s) tradition and to eradicate the insecurities in the hearts of his companions who questioned the validity of their position, where they killed a faction that reveals Islam. When he showcased the hand of Al-Makhdaj, he made them witness that they have fought the faction that the Prophet (s) spoke of. Thus, showcasing the hand of Al-Makhdaj was a political decision to affirm a religious understanding related to the truthfulness of the Messenger of God (s).

It appears from what preceded that Islam does not encourage severing the heads of the non-believing combating enemies, as well as severing the head of the Muslim and parading it from one land to another.

The Umayyads violated this clear religious ruling. We do not know where the Umayyads derived this method in treating their dead. It could be from the mentalities of the Age of Ignorance that they never abandoned. Or they could have adopted it from foreign nations, specifically the Romans who they emulated in their way of life.

The first violation we know of was committed by the agent of Muawiya Ibn Abi Sufyan, Abd Al-Rahman Ibn Abdullah Ibn Othman Al-Thaqafi, in Mosul when he arrested Amro Ibn Al-Hamq Al-Khuzaei[4] after a lengthy pursuit. He killed him, severed his head, and sent it to Muawiya. His head was the first carried in Islam.[5] We will see that this first will also be mentioned as a feature for the head of Hussain, which will demonstrate that the news of severing the head of Amro and killing him did not widely spread amongst the Muslims.

In Hussain's Revolution, the Umayyad clan and their allies committed the crime of severing and transporting the heads on a wider scale.

Ubaidallah Ibn Ziyad ordered to sever the heads of Muslim Ibn Aqeel and Hani Ibn Urwa, after killing them, and transporting them to Yazid Ibn Muawiya in the Levant. He wrote to him, "…God has allowed us to get a hold of them. I approached them and struck their necks. I am sending you their heads."[6]

Ibn Ziyad killed from the revolutionaries in Kufa: Qais Ibn Mishir Al-Saidawi[7], Abdullah Ibn Baqtur[8], Abd Al-A'la Al-Kalbi, and Umara Ibn Salkhat Al-Azadi.[9] He did not send to Yazid Ibn Muawiya the heads of any of his victims except the heads of Hani Ibn Urwa and Muslim Ibn Aqeel.

* * *

After eliminating the revolutionaries in Karbala, a large number of the martyrs' heads were severed and transported to Ubaidallah Ibn Ziyad in Kufa. They were then sent to Yazid Ibn Muawiya in the Levant. The transporting of the heads was an exhibition to showcase the heads to as many people as possible along the road and in the cities that the caravan of heads passed by.

Here were realize that the number of heads severed and carried did not exceed 78. It is possible that it did not even exceed 70 heads, although the number of martyrs surmounted 120.

Here we inquire:

Why were the heads severed? Was it an initiative form Omar Ibn Saad and his officers or was it based on commands from Ibn Ziyad? What was the principle that was followed in severing their heads? Why were not all the heads severed - because only the heads of Muslim Ibn Aqeel and Hani Ibn Urwa were severed in Kufa and 70 or maybe a few more of the martyers' heads were severed in Karbala? Was the severing of the heads strictly an act of revenge or a political act with a vengeful nature?

It is possible that Omar Ibn Saad personally decided to sever the heads of the martyrs, desiring to garner a higher status with Ubaidallah Ibn Ziyad, after he clearly knew of Ubaidallah Ibn Ziyad's evil desire to pursue retaliation, as far as can be imagined. However, we think it is more probable, relying on what we know about Omar Ibn Saad's servile, tremulous, and cowardly personality, that this action was not initiated by him. We believe he received instructions from Ubaidallah Ibn Ziyad. What supports this opinion is that the severing of the dead Muslim heads was a completely new component in the Muslim culture. Pre-Karbala, it was not practiced except by Muawiya Ibn Sufyan's governor of Mosul when he severed the head of Amro Ibn Al-Hamq Al-Khuzaei, as we mentioned earlier. What leads us to believe that this was a novel component in the Islamic culture at that time was what was narrated in one of the texts by Al-Tabari on the behalf of Zir Ibn Hubaish, "the first head carried on a stick was the head of Hussain, may God be pleased with him and send his blessings on his soul."[10]

What preceded leads us to believe that it is more probable Omar Ibn Saad executed a decree he received and did not initiate the severing of the heads, although we have not found in the texts on the subject a text pertaining to that matter. The letter that Ubaidallah Ibn Ziyad sent to Omar Ibn Saad with Shimr Ibn Thi Al-Jawshan consists of his command to Omar to invite Hussain and his companions to surrender. If he refused, "March to them until you kill and mutilate them, for they are deserving of that. If Hussain is killed, let the horses trample his chest and back. He is a thankless, troublesome, a severor of bonds, and an oppressor. My experience in this tells me that he will not be able to harm after his death. But I must say: if I were to kild him, I would do this to him..."[11]

The letter consists of an order to mutilate and to bruise the chest and back of Hussain under the hooves of horses.

The second command was executed by Omar Ibn Saad precisely based on the direct commands. Ten men completed this egregious assignment; Al-Tabari named two of these men who were from Hadramaut.[12]

As to mutilating the dead, was the intended meaning to sever the heads? If that was it, then it was also executed. However, it was not executed with precision because not all of the heads were severed. We doubt that the intended meaning for mutilating was severing the heads. We believe it is more probable that this conduct was based on a decree, a copy of which did not reach us.

Is it an act of retaliation? No doubt, it is retaliatory conduct prompted by hate as is the case withmutilating the bodies and bruising them under the hooves of horses. However, we believe it is more probable that is was not exclusively retaliatory, such that the only goal was to avenge and quench the thirst of hatred, but rather retaliatory conduct with a political purpose as well.

The Umayyad men, led by Yazid ibn Muawiya, believed that Hussain's Revolution is able to undermine the whole government. They recognized that what we now refer to as the "revolutionary state" was dangerously widespread in Iraqi society, although it needed initiation to be activated and to manifest itself through positions and stances. That is why any movement by of an Islamic nature is able to gather the revolutionary forces and give them the power to accomplish a large revolutionary achievement. Thus, Hussain's Revolution – with its leader being one that has a central moral position in Islamic society – presents a dire danger to the Umayyad regime because of what it can invoke in reactions that can elevate the revolutionary spirit. It can grant revolutionary groups in the Islamic community great hopes of triumph, with the presence of leadership that has great moral stock amongst the Muslims. We also recognize that Umayyad personnel understood that the revolutionary group with Hussain represents, in its majority, men that assumed leadership positions in the tribal communities in the south and north, and have followers that are influenced by their positions.

Therefore, the Umayyad men desired to eliminate any hope that the people had in any revolution succeeding by making an example out of the heroes of the revolution.

They mobilized the largest military force they can organize in that short time to eradicate the small force in Karbala. We have previously stated that the size of the Umayyad army ranged between 20,000-30,000. All of that to tightly besiege the revolutionaries so that no single person can escape and no one can reach them. Moreover, they wanted to guarantee their elimination quickly so that the army itself is not influenced if time is prolonged.

Additionally, they executed retaliatory action that humiliated the martyrs and their women, such as bruising the body with under the hooves of horses and mutilating them, and carrying the women as captives for people in the different lands to view.

The goal of the Umayyad regime from all of this was to eliminate the sanctity that surrounded Hussain and his household. The regime wished to inform the revolutionaries that did not have an opportunity to participate in Karbala's Revolution that the measures that the government will take to protect itself do not have any boundaries and it does not respect any sanctity, sacred person, religious norm, or social norm.

The severing of the heads, transporting them from one land to another, and parading them through the cities, specifically Kufa, is part of this general plan. Additionally, the regime wanted to wipe out the revolution's resources and destroy the psychological immunity of the opposition and make it clear to them that the revolution has been fully terminated. Furthermore, they wanted to dispel any rumors via tangible proofs – the heads of the revolutionaries, the first of which is the head of Hussain.

Therefore, there was a political goal in severing the heads in addition to it being a retaliatory measure. This explains to us why all of the heads were not severed in Kufa and Karbala. In Kufa, Ibn Ziyad severed only the heads of Muslim Ibn Aqeel and Hani Ibn Urwa amongst the other revolutionaries that he killed. In Karbala, only half of the martyrs' heads were severed and transported to Kufa.

The severing of the heads was selective. The severed heads were of the prominent men that had a loyal following with respect to their tribes or cities. This destroys their mass bases, disperses their following, and disables its activity.

Hani Ibn Urwa and Muslim Ibn Aqeel are the most powerful men in the movement in Kufa. Thus, Ibn Ziyad severed both of their heads and sent them to Yazid Ibn Muawiya as tangible proof of eradicating the revolution. As to the others who are laypersons, their heads are meaningless because killing them while their leaders are present does not impact the revolution.

Consequently, Ibn Ziyad was not compelled to sever more than two heads.

Such is the case with the Karbala martyrs. The heads of the servants and laypersons did not mean much for the dissident that opposed Umayyad governance. What paralyzed the revolutionary power and resulted in the psychological defeat of the masses is witnessing its leaders and chiefs slaughtered – with their heads hoisted on spears as tangible proof of their murder.

From that, we understand why the head of Hussain was paraded in the alleys of Kufa. "…Then Ubaidallah Ibn Ziyad installed the head of Hussain in Kufa and made it circulate in Kufa."[13]

Although we do not have text, we believe it is more probable that the heads that were distributed to the tribes, were not randomly distributed. Every tribe took the heads of their prominent men to further solidify its political position with the government and to strengthen the position of its pro-government leader.

ADDENDUM

Al-Ziyara Al-Nahiya

The following is the text of Ziyara of Al-Nahiya Al-Muqadasa *as narrated by Sayyid Ibn Tawous in his book* Al-Iqbal.[1]

I narrate [this Visitation] referring to my grandfather Abu Jaafer Ibn Al-Hassan Al-Tousi; he said Sheikh Abu Abdullah Muhammed Ibn Ahmed Ibn Ayash narrated and said that the Rightous Sheikh Abu Mansour Ibn Abd Al-Mun'im Ibn Al-Numan Al-Baghdadi narrated and said: This came from Al-Nahiya in the year 252 AH on the hands of Sheikh Muhammed Ibn Ghaleb Al-Asfahani – after my father's death and when I was still young – after I wrote to receive permission for the visitation of my Master [Imam Hussain] (a) and the visitation of the Martyrs. The answer came:

In the Name of God the Beneficent, the Merciful

If you want to visit the Martyrs – may God be pleased with them – stand at the feet of Hussain (a), which is the grave of Ali Ibn Hussain (a). Face the Qibla for there are the graves of the martyrs. Point to Ali ibn Hussain (a) and say:

Salutations upon you, oh first victim from the best of progenies from amongst the progeny of Abraham the Friend of God. May God send His blessings upon you and your father who has said 'God kill the people that have killed you my son. What audacity do they have to transgress against the Most Merciful and violate the sanctity of the Prophet (s)! The world may as well end after you.'

It is as if you appeared before him and proclaimed to the disbelievers [in verse]:

'I am Ali son of Hussain (a) son of Ali (a). We – by the House of God – are more deserving of the Prophet (s). I will stab you with the spear until it bends. I will strike you with the sword, defending my father – the strike of a young Arab Hashimite man. By God, the son of the imposter will not rule over us.'

[You did so] until you perished and met your lord. I attest that you are more deserving of God and his Prophet, and that you are the son of God's Messenger, and the son of His proof and His trusted one. God has adjudicated between you and your killer, Murra Ibn Munqith Ibn Al-Nu'man Al-'Aabdy. May God curse him and his partners, and place them in the hellfire, and make us amongst those that will meet and accompany you, and accompany your grandfather, your father, your uncle, your brother, and your oppressed mother. I disavow myself from your killers, and ask God to allow me to accompany you in the eternal home. I disavow myself from your stubborn enemies. The salutations, mercy, and blessings of God upon you.

Salutations upon Abdullah the infant son of Hussain – the one shot with an arrow and killed, drenched in blood; the one whose blood ascended to the skies; the one who was slaughtered by the arrow when he was in his father's arms. May God curse his killer Harmala Ibn Kahil Al-Asady and his progeny.

Salutations upon Abdullah son of the Commander of the Faithful – the one who is heavily tried, the caller for loyalty on the land of Karbala, and the one that was struck every time as he came and went. May God curse his killer Hani ibn Thabeet Al-Hadrami.

Salutations upon Al-Abbas son of the Commander of the Faithful – the one who supported his brother with his own self, while taking for his tomorrow from his yesterday; the one who sacrificed and defended [Hussain (a)]; the one who sought to give him his water; the one with severed arms. May God curse his killers, Yazid ibn Al-Riqad Al-Heeti and Hakim ibn Al-Tufail Al-Taei.

Salutations upon Jaafer son of the Commander of the Faithful – the one who is piously patient; the one who left his homeland and became a stranger; the one submissive to the need [to sacrifice in] battle; the one who would race forward to duel, outnumbered by men. May God curse his killer Hani Ibn Thabeet Al-Hadrami.

Salutations upon Othman son of the Commander of the Faithful – the one named after Othman Ibn Math'aoun. May God curse the one who killed him with the arrow Khawli Ibn Yazid Al-Asbahi Al-Ayadi, and Al-Abani Al-Darami.

Salutations upon Muhammed son of the Commander of the Faithful – the one killed by Al-Abani Al-Darami, may God curse him and multiply his severe punishment. Salutations upon you oh Muhmmed and on your patient Household.

Salutations upon Abi Bakr son of [Imam Hassan (a)] the Pure Master – the one showered with arrows. May God curse his killer Abdullah Ibn Aqaba Al-Ghinwi.

Salutations upon Abdullah son of [Imam Hassan (a)] the Pure. May God curse his killer Harmala Ibn Kahil Al-Asady.

Salutations upon Al-Qasim son of [Imam Hassan (a)] – the one struck on the head and whose armor was looted, when he had called upon his uncle Hussain and his uncle flocked to him like an eagle. [Al-Qasim was] digging in the soil with his feet [as he was taking his last breaths]. Hussain would say, '[May God] distance a faction that killed you, for their adversary on judgment day will be your grandfather and your father.' Then he said, 'it is difficult on your uncle to hear your calls but be unable to answer, or answer you when it is too late as you lie murdered and he would not be able to help you. This is a day where the enemies have increased and the supporters have diminished.' May God place me with you on the day when he gathers you all and grants me the place you will have, and curse your killer Amro Ibn Saad Ibn Nafeel Al-Azadi and burn him in hell and prepare for him a painful punishment.

Salutations upon Aoun son of Abdullah, the son of Jaafer the flying one in the heavens. [He is] the ally of faith and the champion against equals; the one promoting the All Merciful; the one reciting the Quran and repeating its verses. May God curse his killer Abdullah Ibn Qutba Al-Nabahani.

Salutations upon Muhammed Ibn Abdullah Ibn Jaafer – the one witnessing [the battle in] his father's stead; the one who followed his brother and defended him with his body. May God curse his killer Amer Ibn Nahshal Al-Timimi.

Salutations upon Jaafer Ibn 'Aqeel. May God curse his killer Bishr Ibn Khawt Al-Hamadani.

Salutations upon Abdul-Rahman Ibn 'Aqeel. May God curse his killer Amr Ibn Khalid Ibn Asad Al-Juhani.

Salutations upon the martyr the son of the martyr, Abdullah Ibn Muslim Ibn 'Aqeel. May God curse his killer Amer Ibn Sa'sa' (and some have narrated as Asad Ibn Malek).

Salutations upon Abi Abdullah Ibn Muslim Ibn 'Aqeel. May God curse his killer Amro Ibn Sabih Al-Saidawi.

Salutations upon Muhammed Ibn Abi Saeed Ibn 'Aqeel. May God curse his killer Laqeet Ibn Nasher Al-Juhani.

Salutations upon Sulayman the servant of Hussain the son of the Commander of the Faithful. May God curse his killer

Sulayman Ibn Awf Al-Hadrami. Salutations upon Qareb the servant of Hussain Ibn Ali. Salutations upon Munjih the servant of Hussain Ibn Ali.

Salutations Upon Muslim Ibn Awsaja Al-Asadi who said to Hussain after being given permission to depart,

> *'Do we desert you? What excuse do we tell God for not fulfilling our right towards you? No, for by God, I will break my spear in their chests, and strike them with my sword as long as its hilt remains in my hand. And if I do not have any weapons in my hands, I will fight them by launching stones at them until I die with you. I will be the first to [sacrifice] himself and the first martyr from amongst the martyrs to reach his end.'*

By the God of the Kaaba, you have triumphed. May God reward you for your persistence and stance with your Imam. [Hussain (a)] walked towards your dead body and said, 'God have mercy on you O Muslim Ibn Awsaja.' Then he recited, 'There are some among them who have fulfilled their pledge, and some of them who still wait, and they have not changed in the least.' May God curse the participants in your murder Abdullah Al-Thabaabi and Abdullah Ibn Khashkara Al-Bajli.

Salutations upon Saad Ibn Abdullah Al-Hanafi the one who said to Hussain after being given permission to depart,

> *We do not leave you until we are certain that we have preserved the Prophet's (s) [rights in his] absence through*

you. By God if I know that I will be killed then revived then burned and scattered, and this happens to me 70 times over, I will not leave you until I meet my demise in protection of you. And how do I not do that, when it is one death, and an everlasting honor.

Surely you have met your demise in your stance with your Imam. You were granted by God honor in the eternal life. May God make us amongst you the martyrs, and grant us your companionship in the highest levels of paradise.

Salutations upon Bishr Ibn Amr Al-Hadrami. May God reward you for your words to Hussain when he granted you permission to leave,

May the beasts eat me alive if I leave you [so that I will have to] ask the caravans about you [after having] abandoned you despie the scarcity of your supporters! This will never be!

Salutations upon Yazid Ibn Haseen Al-Hamadani Al-Mashraqi, the slaughtered reciter. Salutations upon Omran Ibn Ka'b Al-Ansari. Salutations upon Naeem Ibn Ajlan Al-Ansari.

Salutations upon Zuhair Ibn Al-Qain Al-Bajli, the one who told Hussain after being given permission to depart,

No, by God this shall never happen. Do I leave son of the Prophet (s) besieged by the enemies and I shall be free? May God not show me such a day!

Salutations upon Amro Ibn Qurdha Al-Ansari. Salutations upon Habib Ibn Mudaher Al-Asadi. Salutations upon Al-Hur Ibn Yazeed Al-Riyahi. Salutations upon Abdullah Ibn Umayr Al-Kalbi. Salutations upon Nafe' Ibn Hilal Al-Bajli Al-Muradi. Salutations upon Anas Ibn Kahil Al-Asadi. Salutations upon Qais Ibn Mishir Al-Saidawi. Salutations upon Abdullah and Abdul-Rahman the sons of I'rwa Ibn Harraq Al-Ghafari. Salutations upon John the the servant of Abi Thar Al-Ghafari. Salutations upon Shabeeb Ibn Abdullah Al-Nahshali. Salutations upon Al-Hajaj Ibn Yazid Al-Sa'dy. Salutations upon Qasit and Karsh the sons of Zuhair Al-Taghlibi. Salutations upon Kanana Ibn A'teeq. Salutations upon Thirghama Ibn Malek. Salutations upon Juwain Ibn Malek Al-Dub'i. Salutations upon Amro Ibn Dabee'a Al-Dab'i. Saltuions on Zaid Ibn Thabeet Al-Qaisi. Salutations upon Abdullah and Ubaidallah the sons of Yazid Ibn Thabeet Al-Qaisi. Salutations upon Amer Ibn Muslim. Salutations upon Qa'nab Ibn Amro Al-Nimri. Salutations upon Salem the servant of Amer Ibn Mulsim. Salutations upon Sayf Ibn Malek. Salutations upon Zuhair Ibn Bishr Al-Khath'ami. Salutations upon Badr Ibn Ma'qal Al-Ju'fi. Salutations upon Al-Hajaj Ibn Masrouq Al-Ju'fi. Salutations upon Mas'oud Ibn Al-Hajaj and his son.

Salutations upon Majma' Ibn Abdullah Al-'Aa'ethi. Salutions on Amar Ibn Hassan Ibn Shareeh Al-Taei. Salutations upon Hayan Ibn Al-Hareth Al-Salmani Al-Azedi. Salutations on Jundib Ibn Hijr Al-Kholani. Salutations upon Amro Ibn

Khaled Al-Saidawi, and salutations upon Saeed his servant. Salutations upon Yazeed Ibn Ziyad Ibn Al-Mudaher Al-Kindi. Salutations upon Zaher the servant of Amro Ibn Al-Hamq Al-Khuzaei. Salutations upon Jabala Ibn Ali Al-Shaibani. Salutations upon Salem the servant of Bani Al-Madaniat Al-Kalbi. Salutations upon Aslam Ibn Katheer Al-Azadi. Salutations upon Qasim Ibn Habib Al-Azadi. Salutations upon Amr Ibn Al-Ahdouth Al-Hadrami. Salutations upon Abi Thumama Amr Ibn Abdullah Al-Saedi.

Salutations upon Hanthala Ibn As'ad Al-Shabami. Salutations upon Abd Al-Rahman Ibn Abdullah Ibn Al-Kadn Al-Arhabi. Salutations upon Amar Ibn Abi Salama Al-Hamadani. Salutations upon Abes Ibn Shabeeb Al-Shakeri. Salutations upon Shawthab the servant of Shaker.

Salutations upon Shabeeb Ibn Hareth Ibn Saree'. Salutations upon Malek Ibn Abdullah Ibn Saree'. Salutations upon the wounded captive Sawar Ibn Abi Hameer Al-Fahmi Al-Hamadani. Salutations upon the wounded one with him Amro Ibn Abdullah Al-Junda'ei.

Salutations upon you, best of companions.

Salutations upon you oh patient ones who will be granted the eternal life. May God grant you the status of the righteous ones. I testify that God has revealed to you the unknown and prepared for you the valley [of Paradise] and rewarded you generously. You were not slow in [support of] justice. You are amongst us a select few. And we [pray that we] are amongst your company in the Eternal Abode. Salutations upon you and the blessings and mercy of God.

* * *

The following is the commentary by Al-Majliis on this Ziyara.[2]

This visitation was narrated by Al-Mufid and Al-Sayyid in their books of visitation, as well as by other authors. They deleted the source and included it amongst the the visitations of Ashura. Also, the author of Al-Mazar Al-Kabeer said,

> *The Visitation of the Martyrs in the day of Ashura: Al-Shareef Abu Al-Fath Muhammed Ibn Muhammed Al-Jaafari informed me, on the behalf of the Jurist Imad Al-Deen Muhammed Ibn Abi Al-Qasim Al-Tabari, on the behalf of Al-Sheikh Abi Ali Al-Hassan Ibn Muhammed Al-Toosi.*
>
> *And Al-Sheikh Abu Abdullah Hussain Ibn Haba Allah Ibn Rataba informed me on the behalf of Al-Sheikh Abi Ali, on the behalf of his father Abi Jaafer Al-Toosi, on the behalf of Al-Sheikh Muhammed Ibn Ahmed Ibn Ayash.*

Others have related it similarly. But we related it in the general visitations because there is no evidence in the text to support that this visitation is designated for a specific time.

And know that in the history of this tradition is a conflict because it preceded the birth of Al-Qaem (a) in four years. It could have been related in the year 262. And it is also probable that it was relayed through [Imam Hassan] Al-Askari (a).

AL-ZIYARA AL-RAJABIA

The following is an excerpt from the Al-Rajabia visitation that includes the names of the martyrs. It is related here as stated in the book of Bihar Al-Anwar.[1] Direct yourself to the martyrs and recite;

Salutations upon Saeed Ibn Abdullah Al-Hanafi. Salutations upon Jurair Ibn Yazid Al-Riyahi. Salutations upon Zuhair Ibn Al-Qayn. Salutations upon Habib Ibn Mudaher. Salutations upon Muslim Ibn Awsaja. Salutations upon Aqaba Ibn Sam'an. Salutations upon Burayr Ibn Khudair. Salutations upon Abdullah Ibn Umayr. Salutations uoin Nafi' ibn Hilal. Salutations upon Munthir ibn Mufadal Al-Ju'fi. Salutations upon Amro Ibn Qartha Al-Ansari. Salutations upon Abi Thamama Al-Saedi. Salutations upon John servant of Abi Thar Al-Ghafari. Salutations upon Abd Al-Rahman Ibn Abdullah Al-Azadi. Salutations upon Abd Al-Rahman and Abdullah the sons of Irwa't. Salutions on Saif the sons of Harith. Salutions on Malek Ibn Abdullah Al-Hayeri. Salutations upon Hanthala Ibn Asa'd Al-Shabami. Salutations upon Al-Qasim Ibn Harith Al-Kahili. Salutations upon Basher Ibn Amro Al-Hadrami. Salutations upon Abes Ibn Shabeeb Al-Shakeri. Salutations upon Hajaj Ibn Masrouq Al-Ju'fi. Salutations upon Amrol Ibn Khalaf and Saeed his master. Salutations upon Hayan Ibn Al-Harith. Salutations upon Majma' the son of Abdalllah Al-A'ithi. Salutations upon Naem Ibn Ajlan. Salutations upon Abd Al-Rahman Ibn Yazid. Salutations upon Amr Ibn Abi Ka'ab. Salutations upon Sulayman Ibn Aoun Al-Hadrami. Salutations upon Qais Ibn Mishir Al-Saidawi. Salutations upon Othman Ibn Farwa Al-Ghafari. Salutations upon Ghaylan Ibn Abd Al-Rahman. Salutations upon Qais Ibn Abdullah Al-Hamadany. Salutations upon Ghimr Ibn Kunad. Salutations upon Jabala Ibn Abdullah. Salutations upon Muslim Ibn Kunad. Salutations upon Amer Ibn Muslim and the servant of Muslim. Salutations upon Badr Ibn Raqit and his sons Abdullah and Obaidallah. Salutations upon Ramith Ibn Amro. Salutations upon Sufyan Ibn Malek. Salutations upon Zuhair Ibn Saeb. Salutations upon Kasit and Karsh the sons of Zuhair. Salutations upon Kanana Ibn Ateeq. Salutations upon Amer Ibn Malek. Salutations upon Manee' Ibn Ziyad. Salutations upon Nu'man Ibn Amro. Salutations upon Jallas Ibn Amro. Salutations upon Amer Ibn Jaleeda. Salutations upon Za'ida Ibn Muhajer. Salutations upon Shabeeb the sons of Abdullah Al-Nahshly. Salutations upon Hajaj Ibn Yazid. Salutations upon Juwair Ibn Malek. Salutations upon Thabee'a Ibn Amro. Salutations upon Zuhair Ibn Basheer. Salutations upon Masoud Ibn Al-Hajaj. Salutations upon Amar Ibn Hassan. Salutations upon Jundib Ibn Hujair. Salutations upon Sulayman Ibn Katheer. Salutations upon Zuhair Ibn Salman. Salutations upon Kasim Ibn Habib. Salutations upon Anas Ibn Al-Kahel Al-Asadi. Salutations upon Al-Hur Ibn Yazid Al-Riyahi. Salutations upon Thurghama Ibn Malek. Salutations upon Zaher servant of Amro Ibn Al-Hamq. Salutations upon Abdullah Ibn Biqtir the infant of Hussain (a). Salutations upon Manjih servant of Hussain (a). Salutations upon Suwaid servant of Shaker.

Salutations upon you Saintly Ones. You are the elite that God chose for Abi Abdullah (a) and you are the select that God has nominated. I attest that you have been killed in the way of propagating the truth. You have supported, honored, and offered your hearts with the son of the Prophet (s) and you are the joyful ones that have attained the highest of statures. May God reward you as the best of supporters and brothers; the best of reward as that of those who were patient with their Prophet (s). Glad tidings on what you have been given and on your status. May you be showered with God's mercy and through it shall you attain the honor of the hereafter.

* * *

The following is the commentary by Al-Majliis on this Ziyara.²

The Sayyid, may God bless his soul stated,

> *The number of martyrs stated in the Ashura Visitation is more than what we have here based on a different narration. And their names also differ. It is imperative that*

you know, may God support you with piety, that we have followed what we have seen or narrated and have relayed it in every situation as we found it.

THE SHARED NAMES IN THE TWO VISITATIONS

The Names are listed according to the Arabic alphabet.

1. Anas Ibn Kahil Al-Asadi.
2. Bishr (Basheer) Ibn Amr Al-Hadrami.
3. John servant of of Abi Thar Al-Ghafari.
4. Join (Juwair) Ibn Malek Al-Thabaei.
5. Jundib Ibn Hujair (Hijr) Al-Kholani.
6. Jabala Ibn Ali (Abdullah) Al-Kholani.
7. Al-Hur Ibn Yazid Al-Riyahi.
8. Habib Ibn Mudaher Al-Asadi.
9. Al-Hajaj Ibn Yazid (Zaid) Al-Sa'di.
10. Al-Hajaj Ibn Masrouq Al-Ju'fi.
11. Hayan (Hassan) Ibn Al-Hareth Al-Salmani Al-Azadi.
12. Hanthala Ibn As'ad Al-Shabami.
13. Zuhair Ibn Al-Qain Al-Bajli.
14. Zaid Ibn Thabeet Al-Qais: It is narrated in the Al-Rajabiya Visitation (Badr Ibn Raqit).

15. Zuhair Ibn Bishr Al-Khatha'mi – we think it is more probable that he is the same as Zuhair Ibn Saleem Al-Azady based on Al-Iqbal.

16. Zaher servant of Amro Ibn Al-Hamq Al-Khuzaei.

17. Zaid (Yazid) Ibn Ma'qal Al-Ju'fi – we think it is more probable that he is the same as mentioned in the Al-Rajabiya Visitation (Munther Ibn Al-Mufthel Al-Ju'fy.

18. Saeed Ibn Abdullah Al-Hanfi.

19. Saif Ibn Malek, narrated in the Al-Rajabiya Visitation (Sufyan Ibn Malek).

20. Saeed servant of Amr Ibn Khaled, narrated in Al-Rajabiya Visitation (servant of Amr Ibn Khalaf).

21. Saif Ibn Al-Hareth Ibn Abd Ibn Saree', narrated in the visitation: Shabeeb Ibn Al-Hareth Ibn Saree'.

22. Shawthab servant of Shaker, narrated in Al-Rajabiya Visitation (Suwaid servant of Shaker).

23. Shabeeb Ibn Abdullah Al-Nahshli.

24. Thurghama Ibn Malek.

25. Amro (Amr) Ibn Qartha Al-Ansari.

26. Omran Ibn Ka'ab Al-Ansari. It is narrated in Al-Rajabiya Visitation (Amr Ibn Abi Ka'ab).

27. Abdullah Ibn A'meer Al-Kalbi.

28. Abdullah Ibn I'rwa Ibn Haraq Al-Ghafari.

29. Abd Al-Rahman Ibn I'rwa Ibn Haraq Al-Ghafari.

30. Amro (Omar) Ibn Thabee'a Al-Thub'ee, narrated in Al-Rajabiya Visitation (Thabee'a Ibn Omar).

31. Abdullah Ibn Zayd Ibn Thabeet Al-Qaisi, narrated in Al-Rajabiya Visitation (Abdullah Ibn Badr Ibn Raqeet).

32. Abdullah Ibn Zayd Ibn Thabeet Al-Qaisi, narrated in Al-Rajabiya Visitation (Abdullah Ibn Badr Ibn Raqeet).

33. Amer Ibn Muslim.

34. Amaar Ibn Hassan Ibn Shareeh Al-Taei.

35. Amaar Ibn Khaled Al-Saidawi, narrated in Al-Rajabiya Visitation (Amro Ibn Khalaf).

36. Abd Al-Rahman Ibn Abdullah Ibn Al-Kadn Al-Arhabi. It is most probable that he is the one mentioned in Al-Rajabiya as Abd Al-Rahman Ibn Abdullah Al-Azady, as the name and the father's name are the same.

37. Abes Ibn Shabeeb Al-Shakeri.

38. Amr Ibn Abdullah (Abu Thama) Al-Saedi.

39. Qais Ibn Mishir Al-Saidawi.

40. Qasit Ibn Zuhair Al-Taghiliby.

41. Qasim Ibn Habib Al-Azadi.

42. Karsh Ibn Zuhair Al-Taghilibi.

43. Kanana Ibn Ateeq.

44. Manjah servant of Hussain.

45. Muslim Ibn Awsaja.

46. Muslim Ibn Al-Hajaj.

47. Majma' Ibn Abdullah Al-A'ithy.

48. Malek Ibn Abdullah (Abd) Ibn Saree' (Al-Jaberi). The same as Malek Ibn Abdullah Al-Jaberi in Al-Rajabiya Visitation.

49. Naem Ibn Ajlan Al-Ansari.

50. Nafe' Ibn Hilal Al-Bajly Al-Muradi.

THE NAMES EXCLUSIVE TO AL-RAJABIYA VISITATION

The Names are listed according to the Arabic alphabet.

1. Burayr Ibn Khudair.

2. Hamad Ibn Hamad Al-Khuzae' Al-Muradi.

3. Halas (Jalas) Ibn Amro.

4. Rumaith Ibn Amro.

5. Zuhair Ibn Saeb (Sayar).

6. Zaeda Ibn Muhajer. Can this be a typographical error referring to "Yazid Ibn Ziyad Ibn Al-Mudaher)" (Al-Muhajer)?

7. Zuhair Ibn Salman (Sulayman).

8. Sulayman Ibn Katheer.

9. Salayman Ibn Sulayman Al-Azadi.

10. Sulayman Ibn Aoun Al-Hadrami.

11. Aqba Ibn Sam'an.

12. Abd Al-Rahman Ibn Yazid.

13. Othman Ibn Farwa (Irwa) Al-Ghafari.

14. Omar (Umayr) the son Kunad.

15. Amer Ibn Malek.

16. Amer Ibn Jaleeda (Khaleeda).

17. Abdullah Ibn Baqtur.

18. Ghailan Ibn Abd Al-Rahman.

19. Qais Ibn Abdullah Al-Hamadani.

20. Al-Qasim Ibn Al-Harith Al-Kahili (could he be Qasim Ibn Habib?).

21. Muslim Ibn Kunad.

22. Muslim servant of Amer Ibn Muslim.

23. Manee' Ibn Ziyad.

24. Nu'man Ibn Amro.

A Study and Examination of the Visitations

Source and Authorship

The Visitation Attributed to Al-Nahiya Al-Muqadasa

This narration was narrated by Al-Sayyid Ibn Tawous – Jamal Al-Arifeen, Radi Al-Deen, Ali ibn Moussa ibn Jaafer ibn Tawous, d. 664 AH – in his book titled Al-Iqbal in the rituals of the days and the months, and the supplications and Visitations.

He said:

> *Secion: on what we will relate of visitations of the martyrs on the day of Ashura.*
>
> *I narrate [this Visitation] referring to my grandfather Abu Jaafer Ibn Al-Hassan Al-Tousi; he said Sheikh Abu Abdullah Muhammed Ibn Ahmed Ibn Ayash narrated*

and said that the Rightous Sheikh Abu Mansour Ibn Abd Al-Mun'im Ibn Al-Numan Al-Baghdadi narrated and said: This came from Al-Nahiya in the year 252 AH on the hands of Sheikh Mu-hammed Ibn Ghaleb Al-Asfahani – at my father's death and when I was still young – after I wrote to receive permission for the visitation of my Master [Imam Hussain] (a) and the visitation of the Martyrs. The answer came: In the Name of God the Most Beneficent the Most Merciful. If you want to visit the Martyrs – may God be pleased with them – stand at the feet of Hussain (a), which is the grave of Ali Ibn Hussain (a). Face the Qibla for there are the graves of the martyrs. Point to Ali ibn Hussain (a) and say..."

It is apparent from this text that the visitation that is attributed to Al-Nahiya was delivered to us through the following means;

1. **Radi Al-Deen, Ali ibn Moussa ibn Jaafer ibn Tawous** (d. 664 AH) who is from the great scholars known to be humble, worshipping, and trustworthy.

2. **Abu Jaafer Muhammed Ibn Al-Hassan Al-Tousy** (d. 460 AH), known as 'Sheikh Al-Taefa,'[1] too famous to be mentioned. Ibn Tawous narrated it with its reference to his grandfather Abi Jaafer, and we did not have the opportunity to review the chain of narrators from Ibn Tawous to Al-Sheikh Al-Tousy.

3. **Ahmed Ibn Muhammed Ibn Abdullah Ibn Al-Hassan Ibn Ayash Al-Jawhari** (d. 401 AH). He was a contem-

porary to Al-Sheikh Al-Sadouq. He was from amongst those that were versed in knowledge and literature, had good handwriting, and authored numerous books, ie: Muqtadab Al-Athar Fi Al-Nas Ala Al-Ayima Al-Ithnai Ashar (a), Al-Aghsal, Akhbar Abi Hashem Al-Jaafari, and others.

Al-Sheikh mentioned in his Al-Fahrist, 'He listened and accumulated [knowledge], but became [mentally] incapacitated at the end of life. His father and grandfather were prominent dignitaries in Baghdad.'

Al-Najashi said, 'I saw this Sheikh, and he was a friend of mines and my father's. I listened to much from him. I saw our Sheikhs weakening him, so I did not narrate from him and avoided him.'[2]

4. **Abu Mansour Ibn Abd Al-Muni'm Ibn Al-Nu'man Al-Baghdadi.** We did not find a biography with this name, except what was mentioned by Al-Tastary in Qamous Al-Rijal,[3] who did not add anything to the statement in Al-Iqbal. The great researcher and scholar Agha Bozorq Al-Tahrani mentioned in his biographical entry on Al-Sheikh Al-Tousi that of Al-Tousi's teachers was "Aba Mansour Al-Sukari." He also said: "Sahib Al-Riyad (Riyad Al-'Ulama) said that it is possible that he [i.e. Abu Mansour Al-Baghdadi] is Sunni or Zaidi. I say that our Sheikh Al-Nouri ruled out that he is from the Sunnis, inferring that from narrations

that he relays that are not commonly relayed by the Sunnis. However, he did not refute that he is Zaidi"[4]

Sayyid Muhammed Sadiq Bahr Al-Uloom added to this statement in the introduction of Rijal Al-Sheikh, "it is apparent from the texts of the Sheikh that Abu Mansour Ibn Abd Al-Muni'm is one of the Sheikh's teachers."[5]

Is this the same individual mentioned in the chain of narrations of this visitation? Normally, this would be far-fetched. Between the birth of Al-Sheikh in the year 385 AH and the publication of the visitation during the year 252 AH is 133 years.

In any case, the man is unknown.

5. **Al-Sheikh Muhammed Ibn Taleb Al-Asfahani.** We did not find a biographical entry with this name. Al-Tastari mentioned in Qamous Al-Rijal,[6] the statement in Al-Iqbal and added, "What is meant by Al-Nahiya must be Al-Askari (a) because Al-Hujat (a) was not born in that year. Abu Ghaleb narrated on the behalf of Ahmad Ibn Muhammed on the behalf of Muhammed Ibn Ghaleb, on the behalf of Ali Ibn Fadhal in the signs of the first of the Holy Month of Ramadan in the book of Al-Tahtheeb. What is apparent is that he [i.e. Abu Ghaleb] is Al-Asfahani." We do not see anything to support the claim that it is apparent that he is Al-Asfahani. In any case, the man is unknown.

This is the chain of narrators forthe narratin of Ibn Tawous – and it, as you see, is very weak. It has two unknowns and the weak is Ibn Ayash.

* * *

Al-Majlisi stated in Al-Bihar after he narrated the visitation:

> *The author of Al-Mazar Al-Kabeer stated: the Martyrs Visitation on the day of Ashura: Al-Shareef Abu Al-Fath Muhammed Ibn Muhammed Al-Jaafari informed me, on the behalf of the jurist Imad Al-Deen Muhammed Ibn Abi Al-Qasim Al-Tabari, on the behalf of Al-Sheikh Abi Ali Al-Hassan Ibn Muhammed Al-Tousi. Also Al-Sheikh Abu Abdullah Hussain Ibn Wahba Ibn Rataba informed me, on the behalf of Al-Sheikh Abi Ali, on the behalf of his father Abi Jaafer Al-Tousi, on the behalf of Al-Sheikh Muhammed Ibn Ahmed Ibn Ayash, and he mentioned....*

And this chain of narrators, as you see, ends with Ibn Ayash the weak, and the two unknowns, Abi Mansour and Muhammed Ibn Ghaleb.

The analysis of the chain of narrators thus shows that the narration is weak.

* * *

The date mentioned for the visitation which is 252, does not conform with its reference to Al-Nahiya and what is meant by this phrase is the twelfth Imam from Ahlulbayt. However,

227

Imam Mahdi (a) was born in the year 256 AH or 255 AH and his father Imam Al-Hassan Al-Askari (a) died on the eighth days of Rabih Al-Awal in the year 260 AH.

Al-Sheikh Al-Majliis realized this dilemma. He stated in his commentary on the visitation,

> *Know that the date of this narration is problematic because it preceded the birth of Al-Qaem (a) by four years. It could have been 262, and it is probable that the narration is relayed from Abi Muhammed Al-Askari (a).*

Thus, due to this conflict between the date of the publication of this visitation and its referencing, we have two options.

First, delaying the date of publication 10 years such that the visitation is published in the year 262 AH instead of 252 AH, and as such, it can have its origin back to the twelfth Imam.

Second, dismissing its origin and preserving its date by assuming it's origin was the 11th Imam Abi Muhammed Al-Askari (a).

Al-Tastari has unequivocally adopted this second assumption and said: "…what is meant by Al-Nahiya in this narration must be Al-Askari (a), because Al-Hujjah[7] was not born in that year."[8]

The first option faces the follwoing criticism.

First: Designating the year 262 is not supported by any proof. It is probable that this visitation was published after this date by tens of years.

Second: The term used in the reference is that this visitation was released "in the year two hundred and fifty two by Al-Sheikh Muhammed Ibn Ghaleb Al-Asfahani." The explicit meaning of this statement is that Aba Mansour Ibn Al-Nu'man wrote – after the death of his father – asking for permission in the visitation, and Muhammed Ibn Ghaleb is the one that delivered the letter to the Twelfth Imam. It is also explicit in stating that the answer, including this visitation, came from the Imam through Muhammed Ibn Ghaleb. This contradicts what is known that all of the correspondence and writings that were directed from the Shia to the Imam during the minor occultation were through the ambassadors: Othamn Ibn Saeed Al-Umary, and after him his son Abu Jaafer Muhammed Ibn Othman, then Abu Al-Qasim Hussain Ibn Rooh, and then Abu Al-Hassan Ali Ibn Muhammed Al-Sumary. It is not proven that anyone contacted the Imam – during the minor occultation – through other than these four individuals.

The second option is more acceptable than the first. However, the critique to this is that the term "Al-Nahiya" in the culture of the Imami Shia is an exclusive epithet of the Twelfth Imam – Al-Mahdi Muhammed Ibn Al-Hassan (a) – during the minor occultation. We do not know that it was used to refer to any of the other Imams (a).

There have been other terms such as: "Al-Janaab Al-'Aali," "Al-Hathra," "Al-Majlis Al-'Aali" and other widely spread popular terms to refer to official clergy and administrative positions. It was also used to refer to the wives, mothers, sisters, and daughters of the califs and the sultans.

The spread of these terms in the public culture does not justify the conclusion that this term was used in the specific text by the Shia to refer to other than the Twelfth Imam.

It appears to us that the term "Al-Nahiya" is a term specifically found in the Shia culture. Its development was due to different reasons than what caused the phenomena of titles to come about in the administrative culture and the social norm during the second Abbasids era.

This cultural phenomena developed in the state and amongst the people for honorary purposes due to the foreign cultural influence from one side, and also due to the internal dissolution of the government structure which resulted in the survival of the traditional government framework – the calif and his confidants – without the practice of governance that transferred to others such as the prevailing princes who enjoyed and practiced active governance. The granting of honorary titles became ceremonial after the regime had lost its inner strength. Honary titles would grow more abundant and diverse the more the regime continued to dissolve from the inside.

As to the Shia culture, it seems that the title "Al-Nahiya" developed due to security purposes. The government was determined to kill the Twelfth Imam. It frequently raided the home of Imam Al-Hassan Al-Askari searching for the twelfth Imam, which drove the Imam to hide in occultation. It was necessary for the Shia to communicate with their Imam and thus he appointed representatives, which we mentioned, to be correspondents for the Shia to contact. Under these circumstances the term "Al-Nahiya" was born to refer to the Imam in writing and conversation. This does not contradict the facts that choosing this method to refer to the Imam for security purposes emerged from the spread of this phenomenon in the public culture in society at the time.[9]

This term seems to differ in its initiation from its counterparts in the public culture – it seems to be a specific Shia term. The titles of the caliphs, sultans, leaders, scholars, and authors, which spread in the second half of the Abassids Empire, did not have a mentioning of the term "Al-Nahiya." Al-Qalqashandy wrote in his book Subh Al-A'sha additional chapters in which he researched the topic of titles in its practical applications and also what prevailed during his time, but did not mention the term "Al-Nahiya."[10]

This conflict – which we delved in explaining – invites us to doubt that this visitation was offered by Imam Al-Hassan Al-Askari (a) unless it is proven to us that the term "Al-Nahiya" was used to refer to him as it was used to refer to the Twelfth Imam (a).

And as such, we are not able to trace the visitation to Imam Mahdi (a) nor can we believe it is more probable that it was offered by Imam Al-Hassan Al-Askari (a).

At this point, it is imperative for us to research the visitation as a historical text with an unknown author. The author could be one of three persons who were mentioned in the source of the visitation before Al-Sheikh Al-Tousi: Ahmed Ibn Muhammed Ibn Abdullah Ibn Hussain Ibn Ayash Al-Jouhari, Abu Mansour Ibn Abd Al-Mun'im Ibn Al-Nu'man Al-Baghdadi, or Al-Sheikh Muhammed Ibn Ghaleb Al-Asfahani. This is only if the last two are historical figures, and not fictional creations. Or it could be that the author is an unknown man other than those three.

The date of this visitation falls in the latter half of the third century. The origin of the visitation would go back to the Twelfth Imam – even though it was fabricated – so that it can gain the qualities of holiness and authenticity with the believers. This is a means that the fabricators utilized in all of the ages with respect to books, artifacts, and other creations so they can pave the way for their fabrications to spread and be accepted by the audiences they target with their books and texts.

Still, in our opinion, this conclusion does not impact the value of the visitation attributed to Al-Nahiya Al-Muqadasa because it is a primary source for the names of the martyrs of Karbala. The author has good experience with the subject matter, which will be apparent in a later stage of this research.

AL-RAJABIYA VISITATION

Al-Sayyid Ibn Tawous mentioned this visitation in Al-Iqbal[11] without mentioning a source for it. Al-Majlisi relayed in Al-Bihar, after mentioning the Al-Rajabiya visitation, the following words on the behalf of Al-Sayyid Ibn Tawous,

> *The Sayyid mentioned: The number of martyrs stated in the Ashura Visitation is more than what we have here based on a different narra-tion. And their names also differ. It is imperative that you know, may God support you with piety, that we have followed what we have witnessed or narrated and have relayed it in every situation as we found it.*[12]

It seems from this statement that Al-Sayyid Ibn Tawous is the one that authored this visitation, even if he did not announce that.

He admits in this statement that there are fundamental difference between this visitation and the visitation attributed to Al-Nahiya.

It is more likely than not that the Sayyid is the author of this visitation because its history does not exceed more than the end of the second third of the seventh century AH. Sayyid Ibn Tawous died in the year 664 AH.

And from here we cannot consider the Al-Rajabiya Visitation a primary source in our research as we did with the visitation that is attributed to Al-Nahiya, not because we doubt the credibility of Al-Sayyid Ibn Tawous as he is above any doubt, but rather because of our doubt in the accuracy of his sources, and our knowledge in the increased distortions and textual errors as well as the neglect of accurate and scrupulous research during this era.

The Internal Makeup of the Two Visitations

We move with our research to examine the internal makeup of the two visitations. We realize the following;

First: The Number of Martyrs

The visitation attributed to Al-Nahiya contained 63 names. Al-Rajabiya Visitation contained 75 names, including one name that believe is repetitive – it is narrated in Al-Iqbal more than once – which is Al-Hur Ibn Yazid Al-Riyahi. This leaves a sum of 74 names in the Al-Rajabiya Visitation. The increase in the names from Al-Nahiya is by one sixth. However, if we considered the narration in Bihar pertaining to the name we considerably believe is repetitive – Jareer Ibn Zaid Al-Riyahi – the percentage increase in that case becomes more than one sixth.

This phenomena – the increase in the names in Al-Rajabiya Visitation – is not in favor of the visitation because additions to late historical text, without the presence of sources or any considerations for these additions, is a result of distortions and textual errors, as well as an imprecise examination and investigation.

SECOND: SPURIOUS NAMES

Al-Rajabiya Visitation contained the names 'Aaqaba Ibn Sam'an and Abdullah Ibn Baqtur because they are considered to be amongst the martyrs of Karbala.

'Aaqaba Ibn Sam'an was not killed in Karbala. It is more probable that he did not participate in the battle at all. Omar Ibn Saad wanted to kill him when he captured him after the battle. However, 'Aaqaba was released when he informed Ibn Saad that he was a servant of Al-Rabab, the wife of Hussain. He lived many years after that and became a narrator for Hussain's Revolution.

Abdullah Ibn Baqtur did not witness Karbala. He was martyred in Kufa when a representative of Hussain was sent to Muslim Ibn Aqeel before the arrival of Hussain to Karbala. He was captured and killed in the Royal Palace at the command of Ubaidallah Ibn Ziyad.

The visitation attributed to Al-Nahiya did not contain those two names.

Yes, the two visitations shared the mentioning of Qais Ibn Mishir Al-Saidawi who was martyred in Kufa before the arrival of Hussain to Karbala. Thus, he was not amongst the martyrs of Karbala, as was the case with Abdullah Ibn Baqtur.

This comment is not in favor of Al-Rajabiya Visitation because it is indicative of the inexperience of the author in his topic.

THIRD: FAMILIAL ATTRIBUTIONS

The majority of the names mentioned in the visitation attributed to Al-Nahiya are attributed to tribal families. From the 63 men that were mentioned in the visitation, 47 names are attributed to the tribal family that the martyr is supposed to belong to. The names that are not attributed are only 16, which is slightly more than a quarter of all the names mentioned in the visitation.

On the other hand, we find the contrary in Al-Rajabiya Visitation. Only 21 names were attributed by tribe. By contrast, 53 names remained without attribution to tribal families, which is approximately three quarters of the names mentioned in the visitation.

This phenomenon does not favor the Al-Rajabiya Visitation as well. The presence of the name attributions indicates that the author is more experienced in his topic, which makes him more credible when studying this specific text than one who does not have enough expertise in the topic.

FOURTH: ANOMALOUS NAMES

The Al-Rajabiya Visitation contained the name 'Sulayman' five times referring to four men, three of which have the name

Sulayman (Sulayman Ibn Katheer, Sulayman Ibn Sulayman Al-Azady, Sulayman Ibn Aoun Al-Hathramy), and two of which have fathers that are named Sulayman, (Sulayman Ibn Sulayman Al-Azady and Zuhair Ibn Sulayman – based on the Al-Iqbal narration).

This is what raises doubt in the accuracy of the author of Al-Rajabiya or in the accuracy of the sources he used. The name 'Sulayman' was not a widely spread name amongst the Arab Muslim men during the first half of the first century AH. We can confirm that by looking at the indexes of notables in Tarikh Al-Tabari and examining the presence of this name in the men that were mentioned as narrators by Al-Tabari during the desired time frame. We will find that this name was very limited. The same is the case in the book Siffin for Nasr Ibn Muzahim. His index contains nine individuals by this name, not four of which were contemporaries during the era of the Karbala Revolution.

The reason is that names are related to the cultural makeup and conditions of the civilization, which is something that does not change quickly. In fact it changes very slowly. The change occurs when there is a shift in the cultural thoughts and ideas of the nation. These thoughts and ideas must conform to the customs, traditions, names, and hundreds of other cultural elements, both simple and complicated.

The Arabs faced this comprehensive cultural change when they entered Islam where one of the many elements of this new culture are new names that were mentioned in the Holy Quran and the traditions of the Prophet (s). These names conformed with the general notions of the Islamic creed or related back to the old history of Islam, in its previous constructions and the final construction that was sent with the seal of the Prophets (s). This latter line of Islamic names was present in the widely known forms of the Torah and the Bible. However, the Arabs, as we know, did not have a relationship with these two books such that they form cultural thoughts and ideas that are different than what they had during the age of ignorance. Consequently, many entered the Islamic culture carrying names from the age of ignorance and they named their kids with such names, with the exception of the generation that was born after Islam for fathers that lived in the large Islamic centers such as Medina. A few of them carried names related to the foundation of Islamic creed (Abdullah, Ubaidallah, Abdul-Rahman) while the majority of this generation carried names from the age of ignorance or related to it directly or indirectly.

Consequently, it appears to us how the cultural phenomenon of names in every novel cultural system with specific features, does not answer to change readily and quickly similar to other phenomena. Rather it is more conservative and changes very slowly.

We understand – in light of what we presented – that such change requires three or four generations after the society enters a new culture.

The first generation remains carrying the names that originated in the old culture and as such, they name their kids with names compatible with the old culture. There is no doubt that the residue of an old culture and its literature remains live and active, in varying degrees, in the dominant majority of the second generation where their names and their fathers' names originate in the old culture. At the same time they have been fed with thoughts of the new culture. Names related to the new culture come to surface but the names of the old culture remain widely spread, until they start to diminish in the third generation, and parish completely in the fourth or fifth generation.

The Prophet (s) worked to change the widespread presence of names from the age of ignorance in two ways.

First: Issue general instructions to select the likes of Islamic and Quranic names.

Second: Change the names of some of men and women. However, he did not utilize this second approach expansively. Changing the names on a grand scope will disrupt social relations, and will result in a dangerous distortion in the chain of families that the Arabs valued and paid great attention to.

Based on what preceded: If we take into account that in the year 60 AH the base of Arab Muslims comprised of the second generation in addition to the remainder of the first generation, it becomes clear to us that there has not been an opportunity for the new names to spread and replace the old names, specifically the non-Arab names as is the case with the name Sulayman.

Contrary to the situation amongst Arab Muslim, these types of names were widely spread to a certain extent with non-Arab Muslims – those influenced by the Greek culture or those belonging to the Byzantine empire specifically. The reason being that these names mentioned in the Quran and the traditions were familiar to the non-Arab Muslims in their ancient culture.

The visitation attributed to Al-Nahiya contained the name 'Sulayman' once. Furthermore, the name is indicated to be a servant – Sulayman servant of Al-Hussien. Thus, the visitation attributed to Al-Nahiya is compatible, from this aspect, with the prevailing culture of names prevalent during the relevant time period. Consequently, the name Sulayman servant of Hussain is compatible with the nature of things, and not an anomaly as is the case with 'Sulayman' that was mentioned for five presumably Arab men in the Al-Rajabiya Visitation. We must also mention here that Al-Rajabiya Visitation did not contain the name 'Sulayman servant of Hussain.'

The fact that Al-Rajabiya Visitation contained this name – which is anomalous in the Arab-Muslim sphere during that historical time period – in reference to five men is a point of weakness in the visitation.

* * *

These issues that we mentioned invite us to consider the Al-Rajabiya Visitation as a secondary source in its value for the names of the martyrs of Karbala. Therefore, it is impossible to rely on it for the names mentioned exclusively in it. Moreover, it is imperative to corroborate it with another source with respect to any name mentioned in it, after affirming from the source that it did not reference the Al-Rajabiya Visitation.

Thus, the visitation attributed to Al-Nahiya is a primary source for the names of the martyrs because of the time period of its authorship from one aspect, and its immunity from the criticism that we discussed in the Al-Rajabiya Visitation from another aspect.

NOTES

RESOURCES

[1] Maqtal – literally killing or murder – in this context refers to the martyrdom of Imam Hussain and his companions. Hence, books on the Maqtal would be books describing the events leading up to and surrounding the aforementioned martyrdom. –Trans.

THE MAQTAL

[1] 'Ammaribn Khabbab, Abu Mu'awiyah, al-Duhni al-Bajali, al-Kufi. In his *al-Rijal*, Shaykh al-Tusi counted him among the companions of Imam al-Sadiq. Shaykh al-Tusi also mentioned him in his *al-Fihrist* (al-Haydariyyah Press – Najaf / Second Edition) on page 144, and said, "He has a book that Ibn al-Nadim mentioned." In his *al-Taqrib*, Ibn Hajar described him as an honest one who is a Shia. He passed away in 133 AH.

[2] This tradition is characterized by its flow, motion and short sentences. It sums up many of the important situations. Al-Tabari cited it in his main history book in three parts (volume 5). It is peculiar that in his book on the Maqtal, *Muthir al-'Ahzan*, Ibn Nama al-Hilli relied on this tradition. Ibn Nama cited the segment in which Imam Hussain requested to go to Yazid in order for Yazid to decide what to do with him (*Muthir al-'Ahzan*, 36). But the nature of matters suffices to expose the lie in claiming that Imam Hussain made such a proposal. Furthermore, there is a text relayed by histo-

rians, including al-Tabari, on behalf of 'Uqbahibn Sam'an. 'Uqbahibn Sam'an, being a servant of Imam Hussain's wife al-Rabab, was an eyewitness in a position that allowed him complete coverage of the truth behind the events. In this text, 'Uqbah exposes the lie of this rumor. I find this rumor is most likely a result of Umayyad and Abbasid fabrication aimed at distorting the pure image of Imam Hussain in the Islamic mindset (al-Tabari, *Tareek Al-Tabari*, volume 5).

THE STANCE

[1] Al-Mufeed, *Al-Irshad*, 218.

[2] Al-Khawarizmi, *Maqtal Al-Hussain*, 1:220. Though some have cited to Al-Khawarizmi regarding the number of companions with Imam Hussain (a) in Karbala, we note that this number is indicative of those who accompanied the Imam (a) when he left Mecca and not necessarily those who stayed with him until the 10th day of Muharram. Al-Majlisi mentions (Bihar Al-Anwar, 44:313), citing to Amali Al-Sadouq, that Imam Hussain (a), "Left with twenty-one of his companions and family members." We can't accept this tradition because it is only rational to reject things that go against what we know of the circumstances. And we know surely that the number of Banu Hashim, the Imam's (a) family members, easily came to the number or even exceeded it.

[3] Al-Tabari, *Tareek Al-Tabari*, 5:385.

[4] Al-Daynawari, *Al-Akhbar Al-Tewal*, 244.

[5] The word 'leaving' here does not simple mean that he departed Mecca; rather, it carried a greater weight since the dissent of the Kharajites against Imam Ali (a) in Siffin. They 'left' in disdain, dismissal and dissent. The Umayyads tried to use the same label and application to Imam Hussain's (a) movement. When Ubaydallah ibn Ziyad first became governor of Kufa, for example, he asked his administrative staff to gather all the names of Kufa's families and tribes including those from Al-Harouriya and Al-Reyb (Al-Tabari, *Tareek Al-Tabari*, 5:359). Al-Harouriya was another name given Kharajites during the Battle of Harouraa'. After Hani ibn Urwa – one of Imam Hussain's (a) companions – was captured and beaten Ibn Ziyad told him, "Have you become a Harouri for the rest of this day? Your execution is justified. Your blood is on your hands." Allamah Dr. As'ad Ali explained the meaning of 'leaving' (*khurouj*) in a

lecture he delivered at the Charitable Association of Culture (Al-Jam'eya Al-Khayriya Al-Thaqafiya) in Shayyah, Beirut during the commemoration of Ashura. The lecture took place on a Monday evening, January 20th, 1975. He discussed the letter Imam Hussain (a) sent to his brother Muhammad ibn Al-Hanafiya. In the letter he said, "I have not left out of discontent or arrogance... I only left to bring reform in the nation of my grandfather..." In this regard Dr. Ali said, "Leaving here means going beyond the statement of departure to actually departing. He expresses this in his usage of the past tense – "I have only left...'"

[6] In a narration by Al-Tabari referencing Abu Mikhnif he states, "from Medina" instead of Mecca. We find this to be most probably incorrect, as we have verified the text provided by Ibn Al-Atheer, *Al-Kamil fi Al-Tareekh*, 3:278.

[7] Al-Tabari, *Tareek Al-Tabari*, 5:398-399, and Ibn Al-Atheer, *Al-Kamil fi Al-Tareekh*, 3:278.

[8] Al-Daynawari, *Al-Akhbar Al-Tiwal*, 248. It seems that this was widespread during those days even amongst some of the Shia, that the caliphate would go to the Alids or to the Hashimites generally. In a narration by Labta ibn Al-Farazdaq the poet, Abdullah ibn Amr ibn Al-Aass told him during Labta's conversation about his meeting with Imam Hussain (a) in leaving Mecca, "Beware! Why didn't you follow him? He will surely come to rule and raising arms against him and his companions will be forbidden." In the narration, Labta would say, "So I swore to follow him. His statement resonated in my heart. Then I remembered the prophets and how they were killed. That thought prevented me from joining them. The people of the time would say this and continue to wait for him night and day. Abdullah ibn Amr would say, 'The matter will be apparent before the palm trees rise or the little ones grow." (Al-Tabarli, 5:386-387) We notice that many of those who decided to follow Imam Hussain (a) were hinging on the idea that he would come to rule and that raising arms against him and his companions was forbidden. Thus, those with Hussain (a) would inevitably be safe. But when the news came that some of the closest companions of the Imam (a) were killed – meaning raising arms against was not banned as a matter of fact – those people left him.

[9] Al-Tabari, *Tareek Al-Tabari*, 5:419; Al-Ya'qoubi, 2:231; and Al-Khawarizmi, 1:247.

How Many Were They?

[1] Al-Masoudi, *Murouj Al-Thahab*, 3:70 – Al-Mas'oudi mentions in the introduction of his book that he relied on a voluminous stock of historical, geographical, and lineage studies sources. However, he rarely notes the specific sources he used for the details of the events he describes. In regards to this narration, we postulate that Al-Mas'oudi fell victim to misreading between five and five hundred.

[2] Arabs of the time used a united of measurement that is now called the Arabic Mile. It is slightly longer than the modern measurement of a mile. –Eds.

[3] Al-Tabari, *Tareek Al-Tabari*, 5:389.

[4] Al-Tabari, *Tareek Al-Tabari*, 5; Al-Khawarizmi, *Maqtal Al-Hussain*, 1:237.

[5] Mutheer Al-Ahzan, 39.

[6] Al-Luhouf fi Qatl Al-Tufoof, 42.

[7] Al-Tabari, *Tareek Al-Tabari*, 5:392 – 393.

[8] Al-Khawarizmi, *Maqtal Al-Hussain*, 2:4.

[9] Al-Tabari, *Tareek Al-Tabari*, 5:393.

[10] It seems that this phenomenon was present with many, whereby they were empathetic to the movement but physically stood against it in practice. This phenonmenon was accurately illustrated by the words of Al-Farazdaq to Imam Hussain (a), "The hearts of the people are with you and their swords are with the Umayyads." This is something we will discuss in more detail later on, expanding on the presence of a revolutionary sensation within a system that was psychologically paralyzed.

[11] Al-Tabari, *Tareek Al-Tabari*, 5:422. On page 436, Abu Mikhnif mentions the number of cavalry.

[12] Al-Daynawari, *Al-Akhbar Al-Tiwal*, 256.

[13] Tareekh Al-Ya'qoubi, 2:230.

[14] Al-Khawarizmi, *Maqtal Al-Hussain*, 2:4. Al-Khawarizmi predominantly narrates from Tareekh Ibn A'tham, Abu Muhammad Ahmad, who passed away in the year 314 AH. This narration is from that historian, and thus would be a narration in the same standing as Al-Tabari.

[15] Al-Irshad, 233.

[16] The names that we have found by the end of this study, evidencing the number historical men that we are confident were martyred with Imam Hussain (a) in Karbala, total a number of eighty-one names including three servants of the Imam (a). It is mentioned in Ibn Shahr Ashoub 4:113, that ten of Imam Hussain's (a) servants and two of Imam Ali's (a) servants were martyred in the first offensive in the battle of Karbala. Nine remained after that. We cannot ascertain that the twenty-nine names that appeared in the second table of men are conjured. Rather, we are confident that the table has a small number of actual historical individuals even though we can't necessarily pick them out name by name.

[17] Al-Khawarizmi, *Maqtal Al-Hussain*, 2:9; Bihar Al-Anwar, 45:12, relating this from Muhammad ibn Abi Talib Al-Mousawi.

[18] Al-Manaqib, 4:113.

[19] Al-Masoudi, *Murouj Al-Thahab*, 3:71.

[20] Ibid.

[21] This racist mentality has been illustrated by many poetic texts and novels produced by old Arabic literature. An example of this mentality is shown in an incident with Sewar ibn Abdullah ibn Qudama – the judge of Basra – narrated by Abu Ja'far Al-Mansour. A nomad Arab from the tribe of 'Anbar came to the judge and said, "My father died, leaving my brother and I…" He drew two lines in the sand and then said, "And a *Hajeen* (son from a slave-woman)… So how do we split the money?" Siwar replied, "Is there another inheritor other than you all?" "No," the nomad said. "Then the money is split equally between you three." "I don't think you understood me. My father left my brother and me, and the son of slave-woman," said the nomad. Siwar repeated, "The money is split equally between you three." The nomad replied, "The *Hajeen* takes just as my brother and I take?" "Yes!" Siwar answered. The nomad grew angry and insulted Siwar… (Al-Mubrid, Al-Kamil, 2:48). Being born from a slave or a servant killed brotherhood here. And even if this story was fabricated, it gives a clear representation of the prevalent mentality that existed during the second century after *Hijra*. Therefore, it should be no surprise that people at the time of the battle of Karbala, 60 AH, would not include the non-Arab martyrs in their count of Imam Hussain's (a) supporters.

[22] Al-Khawarizmi, *Maqtal Al-Hussain*. Ibn Tawous, *Al-Luhouf fi Qatl Al-Tufouf*. Al-Majlisi also mentions this narration in Bihar Al-Anwar, 44:394, just as Al-Sayyid Al-

Ameen relates this in A'yan Al-Shi'a, 4:110, which we presume he took from Al-Luhouf as well. Ibn Nama Al-Hilli says in Mutheer Al-Ahzan on page 38, "And then came to them a group of the supporters of Umar ibn Saad..." The Late Sayyid Abdel-Razzaq Al-Muqarrem (d. 1972) mentions in his book *Maqtal Al-Hussain*, that the narration is present in two other sources as well: Al-Thahabi, Sayr A'lam Al-Nubala, 3:210, which we were not able to verify due to the book not being available to us, and Tareekh Al-Ya'qoubi, 3:210. Most certainly the Late Muqarrem was mistaken with regards to referencing Al-Ya'qoubi because the narration is not mentioned anywhere in his historical writings.

[23] Al-Tabari, *Tareek Al-Tabari*, 5:431. Take a look at the conversation between Ayoub ibn Mushrih Al-Kheywani and Abu Al-Widak in Al-Tabari, *Tareek Al-Tabari*, 5:437

[24] Al-Tabari, *Tareek Al-Tabari*, 5:455-456; Mutheer Al-Ahzan, 65; Al-Lufouf fi Qatl Al-Tufouf, 60

[25] Al-Daynawari, *Al-Akhbar Al-Tiwal*, 259. Al-Daynouri also mentions, in his relaying of the details of how the heads were passed out amongst the tribes, that the number of severed heads was seventy-five. We will discuss this further below.

[26] Al-Irshad, 243.

[27] Bihar Al-Anwar, 45:62; Al-Luhouf fi Qatl Al-Tufouf, 60

[28] Al-Tabari, *Tareek Al-Tabari*, 5:467-468. It seems that Ibn Shahr Ashoub accepted this narration also, because he narrates from Abu Mikhnif in his book (Al-Manaqib, 4:122) without any objection.

[29] Al-Daynawari, *Al-Akhbar Al-Tiwal*, 259.

[30] Bihar Al-Anwar, 45:62.

[31] Al-Tabari, *Tareek Al-Tabari*, 5:455. Al-Mas'oudi agrees with the number of dead from the Umayyad camp mentioned by Muhammad ibn Muslim. He said, "The number of dead from the supporters of Umar ibn Saad in the battle with Hussain was eighty-eight men..." Al-Masoudi, *Murouj Al-Thahab*, 3:72.

[32] Al-Masoudi, *Murouj Al-Thahab*, 3:71.

[33] Al-Tabari, *Tareek Al-Tabari*, 5:459-460.

[34] Ibid, 5:469.

[35] Ibid, 5:418, 444-445.

[36] Ibid, 5:454. 'Aqaba ibn Sam'aan narrated much of the scenes of Karbala, many of which are narrated in Al-Tabari.

[37] Ibid, 5:454.

[38] Ibid, 5:389.

[39] Al-Khawarizmi, *Maqtal Al-Hussain*, 2:4.

[40] Al-Daynouri, Al-Akbar Al-Tiwal, 256; Al-Tabari, *Tareek Al-Tabari*, 5:422; Shaykh Al-Mufid, Al-Irshad, 233; also the narration by Al-Husseyn ibn Abdul-Rahman that states the presence of the Hashimites in the mobilized fighting force of Imam Hussain (a) on the morning of the 10th of Muharram – Al-Tabari, *Tareek Al-Tabari*, 5:392.

[41] Al-Khawarizmi, *Maqtal Al-Hussain*, 1:243-244; Bihar Al-Anwar, 44:386-387

[42] "... The cavalry (that prevented the tribesmen from Banu Asad from joining the camp of Hussain) came back until it reached the Furat. They stood as a barrier between Hussain and his companions and the water. Thirst overcame Hussain and those with him." Al-Khawarizmi, *Maqtal Al-Hussain*, 1:243-244; Bihar Al-Anwar, 44:386-387.

[43] Al-Tabari, 5:449. Ibn Nama Al-Hilli mentions the name of this soldier in Mutheer Al-Ahzan, 53, to be Zar'a ibn Abaan ibn Darim. Ibn Nama's narration states that the soldier said, "Don't let him reach the water," but does not mention the phrase, "Don't let his Shia reach him."

WHO WERE THEY?

[1] The names are arranged in alphabetical order in accordance to the Arabic alphabet.

THE MARTYRS OF KARBALA

[1] Al-Tabari, *Tareek Al-Tabari*, 5:469.

[2] Bihar Al-Anwar, 45:69.

[3] Al-Rijal, 74.

[4] A'yan Al-Shia, 4:126.

[5] An honorary reference used to address the Late Grand Ayatullah Sayyid Abul-Qassem Al-Khoei by many of his students. Al-Sayyid Al-Ustath means, "Our Honorable Teacher." –Trans.

[6] Mu'jam Rijal Al-Hadeeth: 3:86.

[7] Al-Khawarizmi, *Maqtal Al-Hussain*, 2:24; Bihar Al-Anwar, 45:30; Al-Manaqib, 4:104, except that he said, "and then came forth a young Turkish servant for Al-

Hur…" He is most definitely speaking about Aslem, the man of our discussion here, because every other detail in his story is the same.

[8] Al-Tabari, *Tareek Al-Tabari*, 5:357-358; Bihar Al-Anwar, 44:337-339, 340; Al-Khawarizmi, *Maqtal Al-Hussain*, 1:199. His kunya was mentioned in Bihar Al-Anwar.

[9] Al-Rijal, 4 and 71. He is also mentioned by Ibn Hajar in *Al-Isaaba fe Ma'rifet Al-Sahaba*, by Ibn Abdul-Burfe in Al-Iste'aab, and by Al-Jazari in Asad Al-Ghaba who specifically discusses his death alongside Imam Hussain (a).

[10] Mu'jam Rijal Al-Hadith, 3:232.

[11] Mu'jam Rijal Al-Hadith, 3:233.

[12] Al-Manaqib, 4:102; Al-Khawarizmi, *Maqtal Al-Hussain*, 2:18

[13] Bihar Al-Anwar, 45:24-25.

[14] Muhammad ibn Saad, Al-Tabaqat, 6:58

[15] Al-Manaqib, 4:103.

[16] Al-Khawarizmi, *Maqtal Al-Hussain*, 2:19.

[17] Al-Tabari, *Tareek Al-Tabari*, 5:429-430, 436, 438.

[18] Ibid, 5:421,423.

[19] Al-Luhouf fi Qatl Al-Tufouf

[20] Bihar Al-Anwar, 45:15; the typographical error is located in volume 44 on page 320.

[21] Mu'jam Rijal Al-Hadith, 3:289

[22] Al-Tabari, *Tareek Al-Tabari*, 5:432.

[23] Ibid, 5:444.

[24] Bihar Al-Anwar, 45:70.

[25] Mu'jam Rijal Al-Hadith, 3:314.

[26] Al-Luhouf, 39-40.

[27] Al-Tabari, *Tareek Al-Tabari*, 5:446.

[28] Al-Rijal, 72.

[29] Mu'jam Rijal Al-Hadith, 4:166.

[30] Mu'jam Rijal Al-Hadith, 6:308.

[31] Bihar Al-Anwar, 45:72.

[32] Al-Manaqib, 4:113.

[33] Bihar Al-Anwar, 45:72.

[34] Al-Manaqib, 4:113.

[35] Mu'jam Al-Rijal 4:34.

[36] Al-Manaqib, 4:1014.

[37] Al-Khawarizmi, *Maqtal Al-Hussain*, 2:21.

[38] Bihar Al-Anwar, 45:28.

[39] Al-Rijal, 72.

[40] Bihar Al-Anwar, 45:82.

[41] Mu'jam Al-Rijal 4:173.

[42] Bihar Al-Anwar 45:22,71.

[43] Al-Rijal, 72.

[44] Al-Khawarizmi, *Maqtal Al-Hussain*, 1:237 and 2:19.

[45] Al-Tabari, *Tareek Al-Tabari*, 5:420.

[46] Al-Manaqib, 4:103.

[47] Al-Rijal, 72.

[48] Al-Tabari *Tareek Al-Tabari*, 5:352.

[49] Ibid, 5:440.

[50] Bihar Al-Anwar, 45:71.

[51] Mu'jam Al-Rijal, 4:240.

[52] Al-Tabari, *Tareek Al-Tabari*, 5:401.

[53] Bihar Al-Anwar, 44:376 and 45:72.

[54] Al-Khawarizmi, *Maqtal Al-Hussain*, 2:20.

[55] Al-Manaqib, 4:103.

[56] Al-Rijal, 73.

[57] Mu'jam Al-Rijal, 4:239.

[58] Ibid.

[59] Al-Tabari, *Tareek Al-Tabari*, 5:422.

[60] Ibid, 5:400.

[61] Ibid, 5:327.

[62] Al-Luhouf fi Qatl Al-Tufouf, 32; and Mutheer Al-Ahzan.

[63] Al-Khawarizmi mentions in *Maqtal Al-Hussain*, 2:10, that Al-Hur joined the camp of Imam Hussain (a) with his Turkish servant; however, we have not come to see evidence to conclude that the young servant fought or was martyred to include him in the list of martyrs.

[64] Al-Manaqib, 4:113.

[65] Al-Rijal, 73

66 Mu'jam Al-Rijal, 4:144.

67 Bihar Al-Anwar, 45:43, 73.

68 Maqtal Al-Hussain, 2:24.

69 Al-Tabari, *Tareek Al-Tabari*, 5:443.

70 Al-Rijal, 73.

71 Al-Manaqib, 4:101.

72 Maqtal Al-Hussain, 2:14.

73 Bihar Al-Anwar, 45:18.

74 Al-Manaqib, 4:113.

75 Bihar Al-Anwar, 45:72.

76 Mu'jam Rijal Al-Hadith, 7:215.

77 Bihar Al-Anwar, 45:72.

78 Al-Manaqib, 4:113.

79 Bihar Al-Anwar, 45:71.

80 Al-Tabari, *Tareek Al-Tabari*, 5:396-397.

81 Ibid, 5:426.

82 Ibid, 5:422.

83 Mu'jam Rijal Al-Hadith, 3:266.

84 Bihar Al-Anwar 45:72.

85 Ibid.

86 Al-Manaqib, 4:101.

87 Bihar Al-Anwar, 45:18.

88 Al-Rijal, 74.

89 Al-Tabari, *Tareek Al-Tabari*, 5:445.

90 Bihar Al-Anwar, 45:72.

91 Al-Tabari, *Tareek Al-Tabari*, 5:419.

92 Maqtal Al-Hussain, 1:195, 2:20.

93 Al-Manaqib, 4:103.

94 Bihar Al-Anwar, 45:21, 26, 70.

95 Al-Luhouf, 39.

96 Al-Tabari, *Tareek Al-Tabari*, 5:353.

97 Al-Rijal, 74.

98 Al-Manaqib, 4:113.

[99] Bihar Al-Anwar 45:73.

[100] Mu'jam Al-Rijal, 8:322.

[101] Al-Tabari, *Tareek Al-Tabari*, 5:444.

[102] Al-Rijal, 74.

[103] Bihar Al-Anwar, 45:24.

[104] Al-Manaqib, 4:102.

[105] Al-Tabari, *Tareek Al-Tabari*, 5:453.

[106] Ibid, 5:442.

[107] Maqtal Al-Hussain, 2:24.

[108] Bihar Al-Anwar 45: 31, 73.

[109] Bihar Al-Anwar, 45:72.

[110] Al-Rijal, 74.

[111] Al-Manaqib, 4:113.

[112] Al-Tabari, *Tareek Al-Tabari*.

[113] Al-Rijal, 74.

[114] Bihar Al-Anwar, 45:71.

[115] Al-Tabari, *Tareek Al-Tabari*, 5:443-444.

[116] Al-Rijal, 75.

[117] Maqtal Al-Hussain, 2:22.

[118] Bihar Al-Anwar, 45:28, 29, 73.

[119] Al-Rijal, 75.

[120] Al-Manaqib 4:113.

[121] Bihar Al-Anwar 45:71.

[122] Al-Tabari, *Tareek Al-Tabari*, 5:443.

[123] Al-Rijal, 78.

[124] Maqtal Al-Hussain, 2:22.

[125] Bihar Al-Anwar, 45:28, 29, 73.

[126] Al-Tabari, *Tareek Al-Tabari*, 5:355 and Al-Khawarizmi, Maqtal Al-Hussain, 1:197.

[127] Rijal Al-Najashi, 78.

[128] Al-Rijal, 77.

[129] Bihar Al-Anwar, 45:72.

[130] Al-Manaqib, 4:13.

[131] Bihar Al-Anwar, 45:72.

[132] Al-Manaqib, 4:113.

[133] Al-Rijal, 77.

[134] Al-Tabari, *Tareek Al-Tabari*, 5:352, 354.

[135] Al-Manaqib, 4:113.

[136] Bihar Al-Anwar, 45:73.

[137] Al-Rijal, 77.

[138] Al-Tabari, *Tareek Al-Tabari*, 352 and Al-Khawarizmi, Maqtal Al-Hussain, 1:194.

[139] Ibid, 5:423.

[140] Al-Rijal, 77.

[141] Bihar Al-Anwar, 45:1.

[142] Al-Manaqib, 4:102.

[143] Maqtal Al-Hussain, 2:17.

[144] Bihar Al-Anwar, 45:22.

[145] Mu'jam Rijal Al-Hadith, 9:349.

[146] Maqtal Al-Hussain, 2:22.

[147] Bihar Al-Anwar, 45:28 and in volume 44 page 320, he refers to him as Abdullah ibn Abi 'Urwa Al-Ghafari.

[148] Al-Tabari, *Tareek Al-Tabari*, 5:442.

[149] Al-Rijal, 77.

[150] Maqtal Al-Hussain, 2:23.

[151] Bihar Al-Anwar, 45:29, 71.

[152] Al-Tabari, *Tareek Al-Tabari*, 5:429-430, 436.

[153] Al-Manaqib, 4:113.

[154] Maqtal Al-Hussain, 2:8-9.

[155] Bihar Al-Anwar, 45:12-13.

[156] Bihar Al-Anwar, 45:71.

[157] Al-Tabari, *Tareek Al-Tabari*, 5:353-354.

[158] Al-Manaqib, 4:113.

[159] Bihar Al-Anwar, 45:72.

[160] Al-Tabari, *Tareek Al-Tabari*, 5:353-354.

[161] Al-Manaqib, 4:113.

[162] Al-Rijal, 76.

[163] Al-Manaqib, 4:113.

[164] Bihar Al-Anwar, 45:73.

[165] Al-Manaqib, 4:104.

[166] Maqtal Al-Hussain, 2:21.

[167] Bihar Al-Anwar, 45:28.

[168] Maqtal Al-Hussain, 2:21-22 and Bihar Al-Anwar, 45:7.

[169] Bihar Al-Anwar, 45:73.

[170] Al-Manaqib, 4:101.

[171] Bihar Al-Anwar, 45:18.

[172] Maqtal Al-Hussain, 2:14.

[173] Al-Tabari, *Tareek Al-Tabari*, 5:446.

[174] Bihar Al-Anwar, 45:72.

[175] Bihar Al-Anwar, 45:23.

[176] Maqtal Al-Hussain, 2:24.

[177] Al-Manaqib, 4:113.

[178] Bihar Al-Anwar, 45:73.

[179] Al-Rijal, 77.

[180] Al-Manaqib, 4:113.

[181] Bihar Al-Anwar 45:72.

[182] Al-Tabari, *Tareek Al-Tabari*, 5:413.

[183] Al-Manaqib, 4:105.

[184] Bihar Al-Anwar, 45:71.

[185] Bihar Al-Anwar, 45:22.

[186] Bihar Al-Anwar, 45:70.

[187] Al-Tabari, *Tareek Al-Tabari*, 45.

[188] Al-Manaqib, 4:104.

[189] Maqtal Al-Hussain, 2:17 and 1:240 as "Al-Saa'idi."

[190] Bihar Al-Anwar, 45:21.

[191] Al-Tabari, *Tareek Al-Tabari*, 5:369.

[192] Al-Manaqib, 4:102.

[193] Bihar Al-Anwar, 45:25.

[194] Maqtal Al-Hussain, 2:18.

[195] Al-Manaqib, 4:102.

[196] Maqtal Al-Hussain, 2:14.

[197] Bihar Al-Anwar, 45:18.

[198] Bihar Al-Anwar, 45:69.

[199] Bihar Al-Anwar, 45:71.

[200] Al-Manaqib, 4:113.

[201] Al-Rijal, 79.

[202] Bihar Al-Anwar, 45:73.

[203] Al-Rijal, 79.

[204] Al-Manaqib, 4:102.

[205] Maqtal Al-Hussain, 4:102.

[206] Bihar Al-Anwar, 45:24.

[207] Bihar Al-Anwar, 45:72.

[208] Bihar Al-Anwar, 45:71.

[209] Al-Manaqib, 4:113.

[210] Al-Rijal, 79.

[211] Al-Rijal, 5:405.

[212] Al-Manaqib, 4:113.

[213] Bihar Al-Anwar, 45:72.

[214] Bihar Al-Anwar, 45:72.

[215] Al-Manqib, 4:113.

[216] Bihar Al-Anwar, 45:69 and Al-Tabari, *Tareek Al-Tabari*, 5:435.

[217] Al-Rijal, 80.

[218] Al-Manaqib, 4:113.

[219] Bihar Al-Anwar 45:72.

[220] Qamous Al-Rijal, 9:120.

[221] Al-Tabari, *Tareek Al-Tabari*, 5:469.

[222] Al-Rijal, 80.

[223] Bihar Al-Anwar, 45:69.

[224] Al-Tabari, *Tareek Al-Tabari*, 5:404.

[225] Al-Rijal, 80.

[226] Bihar Al-Anwar, 45:71.

[227] Al-Manqib, 4:104.

[228] Al-Manaqib, 4:113.

[229] Al-Rijal, 80.

[230] Al-Manaqib, 4:113.

[231] Al-Rijal, 80.

[232] Bihar Al-Anwar, 45:70.

[233] Al-Manaqib, 4:101.

[234] Maqtal Al-Hussain, 2:12-13.

[235] Bihar Al-Anwar, 44:320-321 and 45:16-17.

[236] Al-Manaqib, 4:102.

[237] Maqtal Al-Hussain, 2:17.

[238] Al-Rijal, 81.

[239] Bihar Al-Anwar, 45:72.

[240] Al-Tabari, *Tareek Al-Tabari*, 5:408, 445-446.

[241] Al-Manaqib, 4:113.

[242] Maqtal Al-Hussain, 2:25.

[243] Bihar Al-Anwar, 45:72.

[244] Al-Tabari, *Tareek Al-Tabari*, 5:408, 445-446, and A'yan Al-Shia 4:100, 115-116.

[245] Al-Tabari, *Tareek Al-Tabari*, 5:353-354.

[246] Bihar Al-Anwar, 45:72.

[247] Mu'jam Rijal Al-Hadith, 3:266.

PRESUMABLY AMONGST THE MARTYRS OF KARBALA

[1] Al-Manaqib, 4:105.

[2] Mutheer Al-Ahzan, 42-43.

[3] Bihar Al-Anwar, 45:30.

[4] Mu'jam Rijal Al-Hadith, 6:205.

[5] Al-Manaqib, 4:113.

[6] Mu'jam Al-Rijal, 6:306, 307. Al-Tustari came to the same conclusion.

[7] Mu'jam Al-Rijal, 7:204.

[8] Mu'jam Al-Rijal, 7:296.

[9] Ibid.

[10] Maqtal Al-Hussain, 2:20.

[11] Mu'jam Rijal Al-Hadith, 8:186.

[12] Al-Manaqib, 4:113.

[13] Qamous Al-Rijal, 6:79.

[14] Maqtal Al-Hussain, 2:9.

[15] Al-Manaqib, 4:104.

[16] Maqtal Al-Hussain, 2:19.

THE COMPANIONS MARTYRED IN KUFA

[1] Al-Tabari, *Tareek Al-Tabari*, 5:369-370.

[2] Ibid, 5:379.

[3] Ibid, 5:398.

[4] Ibid, 5:394-395.

THE HASHIMITE MARTYRS OF KARBALA

[1] Al-Masoudi, *Murouj Al-Thahab*, 3:71.

[2] Maqtal Al-Hussain, 2:47.

[3] Ibid, 2:46-47.

[4] Shaykh Al-Mufid, Al-Irshad, 248-249.

[5] Maqtal Al-Hussain, 2:47.

[6] Maqatel Al-Talibeen, 95.

[7] Maqtal Al-Hussain, 2:47-48.

[8] Al-Khawarizmi, Maqtal Al-Hussain, 2:28-29.

[9] Maqtal Al-Hussain, 2:47-48.

[10] Maqtal Al-Hussain, 2:31-32.

[11] Maqtal Al-Hussain, 2:47.

[12] Maqtal Al-Hussain, 2:48.

[13] Ibid.

[14] Ibid.

BURIAL SITES

[1] Al-Tabari, *Tareek Al-Tabari*, 5:334

[2] Ibid, 5:447-448.

[3] Al-Irshad, 239-240.

[4] Al-Irshad, 243.

[5] Al-Masoudi, *Murouj Al-Thahab*, 3:72.

[6] Al-Ghadhiriya: a village on the Furat River that was named after the Ghadhira clan from the tribe of Asad.

[7] Al-Irshad, 243.

[8] Al-Irshad, 249.

[9] Al-Ha'ir: an Arabic term that literally means 'perplexed' was coined to describe the area directly surrounding Imam Hussain's (a) grave. The term was used after the following occurrence. During the time of the Abbasid empire, the tyrants attempted to flood the grave and remove all signs of his burial place. However, the water miraculously evaded the grave and began to circulate it, as if it were 'perplexed' – the literal meaning of Al-Ha'ir.

[10] Ibid.

[11] A'yan Al-Shia, 4:142.

THE ELITE

[1] A Kufan loyal to the Umayyad regime. He was one of the close ones to Ziyad Ibn Sumayya and participated in the slaying of Hijr Ibn Adi Al-Kindi. He was one of Ubaydallah Ibn Ziyad's confides. Addtionally, he was one of three men that lured Hani Ibn Urwa to Iby Ziyad after discovering the issue of Muslim Ibn Aqeel. His sister was married to Hani Ibn Urwa. In Karbala, he led the forces that percldued Hussain and his companions form the Euphrates water and he was in the right flank of the Umayyad army in Karbala. He was one of the carriers of the heads to Ubaydallah Ibn Ziyad and was one of the ones that wrote to Hussain requesting from him to come to Kufa, writing "...if you wish, come and find mobilized soldiers." Al-Tabari, *Tareek Al-Tabari*, 5:270, 349, 353, 364-365, 367, 422, 456.

[2] Al-Tabari, *Tareek Al-Tabari*, 5:435.

[3] Excelling in the military field was sufficient to inspire others to overcome the look of bigotry against the non-Arab Mawali, and to inspire respect and admiration for a Mawla. See: Al-Kaamil, 3:316-17.

[4] It is certain that this is an Islamic term – meaning the class of people who are conscious of the true teachings of Islam and committed to it with preciseness such that they make principled decisions to address the problems they face in society. They do not stand neutral before these problems but rather express their theoretical commitment through their daily practices struggling against deviancy.

It seems to us from a quick study of this term that it was born early in the Islamic culture, specifically when the deviant forces started spreading their ideas and thoughts and recruiting supporters. Thus, we find it mentioned abundantly in the words of the Commander of the Faithful Ali Ibn Abi Taleb, who was forced to engage in intellectual and militant battles with them when they revealed their true corrupt colors. If he was incapable in defeating them militarily and destroying them completely, and removing them from the circles of Islamic life, he was successful in exposing them intellectually.

This term was mentioned in the sermons, books, and short statements of the Commander of the Faithful Ali to refer to the vigilant ones that confront the unmindful ones, and to express the position of the vigilant ones from temptations or to express the position of the unmindful ones from temptation and fear.

For example, it is narrated in a letter from him to Mu'awiya Ibn Abi Sufyan: "You have misguided a whole generation of men which you have misguided by your trickery and thrown into the tides of your ocean... They transgressed against their [proper] path and turned on their heels... They became haughty in bloodline. Except whoever was guided from the men of wisdom. They left you after knowing you, and they beseeched God rather than support you." Nahj Al-Balagha, Letter 32. Ibn Abi Al-Hadid wrote commenting on this, "(They became haughty in bloodline) meaning that they did not rely on faith, but were misguided by fanaticism and tribal pride that they sought comfort in it rather than religion. Then he made an exception to a group that was guided..." Sharh Nahj Al-Balagha, 16:132-33.

And in another sermon attributed to him, he alluded to coming battles and described the people of misguidance. "Their period became long in order that they might complete (their position of) disgrace and deserve vicissitudes, till the end of the period was reached, and a group of people turned towards mischief and picked up their arms for fighting. The virtuous did not act as if they did a favor to Allah but calmly endured, and did not feel elated for having engaged themselves in truthfulness. Eventually the period of trial came to an end according to what was ordained. Then they put their wisdom in their swords and sought nearness to Allah according to the command of their leader." In this he means the people of the Age of Ignorance in one respect, and the Muslims of the era of the Prophet (s) in another respect.

Ibn Abi Al-Hadeed said in explaining this text, "… Until they gave peace to this group because they cannot fight, and they rested from the fight by entering with them in their misguidance and mutiny… Until God called those courageous sages, and they rose 'and put their wisdom in their swords…' Meaning that they showed their wisdom and their faith to the people, unveiling and unsheathing them, as if they were carried on their swords so that they are seen by whoever can see the swords…" Sharh Nahj Al-Balagha, 9:129-31.

His words, "They put their wisdom in their swords" – to put in other words in our modern language – means that they declared a stance by their principles and struggled in its way.

And in another text from Nahj Al-Balagha concerning the people of wisdom in one of his sermons regarding his battles, he said, "The secrets have been unveiled to those who can se and the path has been cleared for its seekers."

Also amongst them is what he said in a sermon where he described bees and locust, "And if they reflected about the greatness of [God's] omnipotence and the grandure of [His] blessings, they would come back to the path and be in fear of the torture of hellfire. Yet hearts are ailing and judgments are capricious."

And amongst them is his saying when he addressed his companions, "… So implement your judgment and let your intentions be true in your struggle against your enemies. By Him, who there is no god but He, I am surely on the path of truth, and they are on the slope of evil…"

And amongst them is his saying in supplication, "My God, you are the most comforting comforter to your friends… you watch them in their privacy, you peer into their consciences, and you know where their sight reaches.…"

And amongst them is one of his short sayings – "… hopes blind the eye of foresight…"

And this term also appeared in the words of the Abbasid caliph Al-Mahdi, when he said it to his vizier commenting on the stance of a revolutionary in his time which was firm and resolute: "Do you not see his lack of fear and resolve of his heart? By God, this is how the people of foresight are." Maqatil Al-Talibiyeen, 418.

5 Al-Tabaqat, 7:117.

THE ARABS AND THE MAWALI

1 The term Mawla (plural Mawali) is derived from the term that meant servant in such a context. All non-Arab Muslims were considered second class citizens within the Umayyad Empire, and were thus called Mawali, or servants. –Eds.

2 Al-Tabari, *Tareek Al-Tabari*, 5:348, 362. This is in the narration by Amar Al-Dihni and Abi Makhnaf. As to the narration by Isa Ibn Yazid Al-Kinani, this servant did not belong to Ibn Ziyad, but rather he was a servant to Bani Tamim. Al-Tabari, *Tareek Al-Tabari*, 5:360.

3 Al-Tabari, *Tareek Al-Tabari*, 6:361.

4 Muslim ibn Awsaja was mentioned amongst the martyrs. He solicited allegiance for Imam Hussain (a) and was a financial trustee for Muslim Ibn Aqeel in Kufa.

5 Al-Hamra – litteraly 'redskins' – was a name used to refer to Persian Muslim at the time, then used to refer to Roman Muslims.

6 Al-Mubrad, Al-Kamel, 2:62.

7 His father led the Al-Jisr battle at Buwaib in Nukhila, which the Muslims lost to the superior Persians military. He died in the battle. Al-Mukhtar's wife, Amra Bint Al-Nu'man Ibn Basheer Al-Ansari, was killed by Mus'ab Ibn Al-Zubair, after extinguishing Al-Mukhtar's revolution. Al-Mukhtar had a residence in Kufa where Muslim Ibn Aqeel stayed, in addition to an estate near Kufa. Al-Mukhtar announced his revolution in Kufa on Wednesday morning 13 Rabi' Al-Awal, in the year 66 AH (18 October 675 CE). The revolution was terminated when Al-Mukhtar and a group of suicidal companions were killed on the 14 of Ramadan, in the year 67 AH (3 April, 687 CE), when Al-Mukhtar was 67 years old.

8 Al-Mukhtar sent to Medina, in agreement with Abdullah Ibn Al-Zubair, an army comprised of 3,000 Mawali under the command of Sharhabeel Ibn Waras Al-Hamadani, to participate in combating the Levantine army, with Ibn Zubair's army

comprised of 2,000 soldiers under the leadership of Ayash (or Abbas) Ibn Sahl Ibn Saad Al-Ansari. However, in agreement with Abdullah Ibn Al-Zubair, Ayash contrived a massacre for his ally, resulting in the army's massacre.

Northern and Southern Arabs

[1] Al-Tabari, *Tareek Al-Tabari*, 5:373.

[2] Al-Khowariami, Maqtal Al-Hussain 1:187-188.

[3] Al-Tabari, *Tareek Al-Tabari*, 5:383-384, Al-Khorazami: Maqtal Al-Hussain 1/216.

[4] The four men are Jabir ibn Al-Harith (Junada ibn Al-Harith) Al-Salmani, Amr ibn Khalid Al-Saydawi, Majma ibn Abdullah Al-'Ayethi, and 'Ayeth ibn Mujma.

[5] Al-Tabari, *Tareek Al-Tabari*, 5:405-06.

[6] Al-Masoudi, *Murouj Al-Thahab*, 3:93. Hamadan is a tribe from Yemen from the southern part of the Arabian Peninsula. –Eds.

[7] Al-Tabari, *Tareek Al-Tabari*, 5:37. It was mentioned in the text: "… [Ibn Ziyad] despised to send with [Ibn Al-Ash'ath] his people [i.e. the tibe of Kinda] because he knew that every tribe hated to confront someone like Ibn Aqeel." This conclusion from Abi Makhnaf makes the selection of soldiers from Qais based on administrative factors strictly. We realize that Shimr Ibn Thy Al-Jawshan, one of the most prominent Umayyad men in Karbala, was from Qais.

[8] Sulayman Ibn Qita Al-Muhariby is amongst the followers of the companions, a servant of Taim Quraish. Al-Ma'ref, Ibn Qatiba, 487. He is combating a tribe from Fahr Ibn Malek Ibn Al-Nuthr Ibn Kanana who all the tribes of Quraish go back to in ancestry. And from Fahr: Al-Thahak Ibn Qais Al-Fahri, the chief of the Qaisiya during the battle of Murj Rahet against Al-Yemeniya led by Marwan Ibn Al-Hakam during the struggle for the Caliphate after the death of Muawiya Ibn Yazid Ibn Muawiya. The battle ended with the loss of Al-Qaisiya, which paid allegiance to Abdullah Ibn Al-Zubair, and the death of Al-Thahak Ibn Qais Al-Fahri.

[9] Al-Mubrad (Abu Al-Abbas Muhammad ibn Yazid): Al-Kamil, 1:223.

[10] Al-Tabari: 5/378-379, 397. "…I saw them being dragged by their feet in the market."

[11] Al-Tabari, *Tareek Al-Tabari*, 5:398.

[12] Al-Tabari, *Tareek Al-Tabari*, 5:395.

[13] We believe the Umayyad army in Karbala exceeded 4,000, which is a number generally accepted by historians. It is narrated by Al-Turmah Ibn Uday in his discussion with Hussain when he met him at the Udayb Al-Hujanat, "…The day before I left Kufa, I saw a massive amount of people that I have never witnessed before. I asked about them and was told: they met to display, then proceed to Hussain…" Al-Tabari, *Tareek Al-Tabari*, 5:406. The books of Maqtal mention narrations that state the number of soldiers in the Umayyad army. The closest number to reality ranged between 20,000 and 30,000.

HASHEMITES, TALIBIDS, AND ABBASIDS

[1] The Talibids is an indication to the sons of the uncle of the Prophet (s), Abu Talib ibn Abdul-Muttalib ibn Hashim. –Eds.

[2] "…When Ibn Abbas left from Hussain, he passed by Abdullah Ibn Al-Zubair, and said: congratulations O Ibn Al-Zubair. Then he said [in verse], 'What a skylark you are in a plentiful valley / the field is open for you, so be white or yellow as you wish / and peck whatever it is you wish to peck.' He continued, 'This is Hussain leaving towards Iraq, so now you have Hijaz.'" Al-Tabari, *Tareek Al-Tabari*, 5:384.

[3] We remember here when Abdullah Ibn Abbas embezzled the funds from the treasury of Basra when he was the governor, appointed by Imam Ali Ibn Abi Talib (a). We remember his brother, Ubaidallah Ibn Abbas, and his support for Muawiya's camp due to temptations, and abandoning Imam Hassan (a) although he was one of his top commanders.

[4] The widespread historical account is as follows: The Kaysanites used to believe in the Imamate of Muhammad the son of Imam Ali Ibn Abi Talib (known as Ibn Al-Hanafiyya). After the death of Muhammad Ibn Al-Hanafiyya, their allegiance shifted to his son Abi Hashem Abdullah Ibn Muhammad. Abi Hashim was eloquent and persuasive. Sulayman Ibn Abd Al-Malek summoned him to Damascus (or Abi Hashem went to him) where he hosted him and treated him well. But Sulayman decided on killing him because he feared him. He poisoned him when he was on his way to Al-Shurat Province in the year 68 AH.

When Abu Hashim felt death, he veered to Al-Hamima (a village near Al-Aqaba) where Ali Ibn Abdullah Ibn Abbas and his son resided and declared to them their right in Imamate. He revealed to them the name of the head propagator in Kufa and his deputy propagators in various parts. Additionally, he provided them with books to be delivered to those propagators. This occurred in the year 99 AH.

With this this, the right of caliphate switched from the Alids to the Abbasids. The allegiance of the Kaysanites also transferred to them. After the death of Ali Ibn Abdullah, the Abbasid Muhammad Ibn Ali, who died in the year 125 AH, took over the task of calling. During his tenure, Abu Muslim Al-Khorsani became one of the propagators. Muhammad Ibn Ali Ibn Abdullah Al-Abbasi handed down this affair to his son Ibrahim, known as Al-Imam, who was responsible for assigning Abu Muslim as the head propagator Khorasan. Marwan Ibn Muhammad (Al-Himar) captured Ibrahim in Al-Hamima and imprisoned him in Haran, where he died. When Ibrahim realized his fate, he bequeathed his authority to Abi Al-Abbas Al-Saffah and commanded him to depart with his family to Kufa. Abu Salma Al-Khalal, the head propagator, received them and placed them in a secret home, until the Abbasid government was announced with allegiance given to Abi Al-Abbas Al-Saffah on the 12 of Rabi' Al-Awal, 132 AH. We have our doubts about this narration. It raises many questions that cannot be answered, starting with the relationship between Muhammad Ibn Al-Hanifiya and his son Abi Hashem from one aspect and between the Kaysanite faction from another aspect. What is strange is that this faction lost its massive role in the development of events as soon as Abi Hashem relinquished authority. Why didn't Abi Hashem entrust his affairs with one of Ali's sons and what are the proofs that make the propagation of the Abbasids for this relinquishment trustworthy?

[5] Abu Salma Al-Khalal (Hafs Ibn Sulayman) was appointed by Bakeer Ibn Mahan as his successor in leading the propagators in Kufa. Bakeer wrote to Muhammad Ibn Ali Ibn Abdullah Ibn Abbas about that and Muhammad wrote to Abi Salma and assigned him the propagation after the death of Bakeer Ibn Mahan.

Abu Salama was a servant of Bani Harith Ibn Ka'ab. He was raised in Kufa and sold vinegar, thus he was nicknamed Al-Khalal. He was a proficient persuader and had a talent for administration, which he attained from his successful secretive work against the Umayyad clan.

When Ibrahim Ibn Muhammad (Al-Imam) was killed in his prison in Haran, his brothers, Abu Jaafer (Al-Mansour) and Abu Abbas (Al-Saffah) feared for their lives so they left Al-Hamima with some of the Abbasid men, escaping to Iraq. They arrived to

Kufa and went to Abi Salma Al-Khalal who hid them in one of the Shia homes in Kufa.

When the allegiance was given to Abi Al-Abbas Al-Saffah, he appointed Abi Salma the propagator to take care of all affairs and made him his minister. Thus, he became known as the Minister of the Household of Muhammad (s). He used to execute without being commanded. However, Al-Saffah discovered Abi Salma's political change of heart to the Alids. Abu Muslim and Abu Jaafer Al-Mansour conspired to kill Abi Salma. Al-Saffah's position regarding the murder of Abi Salma remains unkown. However, there is not doubt that Al-Saffah's confidants had a hand in conspiring for his murder. Abu Muslim sent Marwan Al-Daby, one of his associates, and instructed him: "Go to Kufa. Take Abu Salama from Imam Abi Abbas, kill him, and leave immediately." Al-Duby did just that. Abu Muslim did this based on Al-Saffah and his associates' desire. Al-Daynawari, *Al-Akhbar Al-Tawal*, 334, 358-359, 370. Al-Masoudi, *Murouj Al-Thahab*, 3:268, 284.

[6] We do not know the motivation that drove Abu Salma Al-Khalal to shift his loyalty from the Abbasids to the Alids before the announcement of the Abbasid government. When Abu Jaafer and Abu Al-Abbas sought Kufa, Abu Salma hosted them at Al-Walid Ibn Saad's residence and entrusted them with Musawir Al-Qasab and Yaqteen Al-Abazari, who were two of the prominent Shia (Abbasid Shia??). He isolated them from people and wrote letters to Imam Jaafer Al-Sadiq, Omar Al-Ashraf the son of Imam Zein Al-Abideen, and Abdullah Al-Mahath. Then, he ordered his messenger (Muhammad Ibn Abd Al-Rahman Ibn Aslam) to find Imam Al-Sadiq and deliver the letter. If the Imam complies with the message, Muhammad should not deliver the other two messages. If the Imam doesn't comply, he should attempt with Abdullah Al-Mahath. If he too did not compye, then he should attempt with Omar Al-Ashraf.

The messenger met Imam Jaafer and delivered the letter. The Imam said, "why should I agree to Abu Salama's request when he is a follower of another group." The messenger requested from the Imam to read the letter. The Imam asked his servant, to bring the lantern. The servant brought the lantern to the Imam who placed the letter in the lantern and burned it. The messenger told the Imam, "will you not answer him?" The Imam replied, "you have witnessed the answer, inform your friend what you have observed." The messenger then met Abdullah Ibn Mahath Ibn Imam Al-Hassan Ibn Ali who was delighted by Abi Salma's letter. Abdullah had a contentious discussion with

Imam Al-Sadiq who prohibited him from accepting Abu Salma's offer. Ibn Qatiba, Al-Imamate Wal Siyasa, 2:152-153, 155-156; Al-Masoudi, *Murouj Al-Thahab*, 3:268-269, 284-285.

There is an accusation directed to Abu Muslim Al-Khorasani himself that he attempted to lure Imam Al-Sadiq (a) to agree to transfer governance to him. He wrote to the Imam saying: "I have revealed the word, and called upon the people to stop following the Umayyads and to follow Ahlulbayt. If you agree, it is yours and no one will supersede you." The Imam replied, "You are not one of my men, and this is not my time." Al-Malal Wa Al-Nahal.

THE YOUTH AND ELDERS

[1] Al-Tabari, *Tareek Al-Tabari*, 5:371.

KUFA, BASRA, AND HIJAZ

[1] Al-Tabari, *Tareek Al-Tabari*, 5:357-358.

[2] Ibid, 5:353-354.

[3] There were many conflicts between the people of Basra and Kufa over which province has a greater right to the revenues of a conquered land. For example, in the year 22 AH, Omar Ibn Suraqa, governor of Basra, wrote to Omar Ibn Al-Khattab and mentioned to him the increase of the people of Basra and the inadequacy of its revenues. He requested for the income of either Mahein or Masabathaan to be given to them. This was conveyed to the people of Kufa so they told Ammar Ibn Yasir, governor of Kufa, "Give us authority over the towns of Ramhirmuz and Aythaj and exclude [the Basrans]. They did not help us [against these towns] and they did not join [our army] until we conquered [them]." There was a rivalry between the two cities until it was ended by Omar ibn Al-Khattab. Al-Tabari, *Tareek Al-Tabari*, 4:160-62.

These conflicts repeated between Kufa and Basra numerous times. Al-Tabari referred to them in more than one occasion in his history.

[4] Al-Tabari, *Tareek Al-Tabari*, 5:323.

[5] Omar Ibn Al-Khatab said, "Iraq has the treasury of faith. They are the spear of God. They satisfy the [needs of] the borders [for guardians] and suffice the lands." He means Kufa. See: Ibn Saad, Al-Tabaqat, 6:1 and on.

[6] Hassan Ibrahim Hassan: Tarikh Al-Islam 1/517, 518. Kufa would always determine political outcomes. Afterall the people of Kufa are 'the head of the Arabs,' ;the skull of the Arabs,' sthe skull of Islam,' and 'the dome of Islam.' Omar would start with the people of Kufa. In it were homes of all the Arab, and not in Basra. See: Al-Tabaqat 6:1-6.

THE DEGREE OF THE REVOLUTIONARY STATE

[1] Al-Tabari, *Tareek Al-Tabari*, 5:371.

[2] Ibid, 5:359.

[3] Ibid, 5:363.

[4] Ibid, 5:395-396.

[5] The Arabs of the time often used the name of the Grand Mosque to mean the city of Mecca in general. –Eds.

[6] 351.

[7] The battle of Al-Warda (Head of Ayn) was by the Al-Tawaboun, led by Sulayman Ibn Sarad Al-Khazaei. They were four thousand against Ubaidallah Ibn Ziyad who came with a massive army from the people of the Levant to reclaim Iraq under the Umayyad rule, which assigned Marwan Ibn Al-Hakam as the Caliph. The battle commenced on Wednesday, 22 of Rabi' Al-Thani, 65 AH (Wednesday 3 January 685 CE).

[8] Note: Al-Tabari, *Tareek Al-Tabari*, 5:437.

THE POLITICAL SIGNIFICANCE OF SEVERING HEADS

[1] "Malek Ibn Nuwaira was one of the most hairy people. The military personnel (militants of Khaled Ibn Al-Waleed) used the heads as beds for the pots (they placed the

heads as beds for the pots and ignited the fire under them for cooking). Every single head was scorched by fire except the head of Malek. The food in the pot was cooked, but his head did not due to his plentiful hair." Al-Tabari, *Tareek Al-Tabari*, 3:279.

[2] When it was the day of Nahr, Ali proclaimed, "Go find Al-Makhdaj." They searched for him unsuccessfully, disappointing Ali. Then a man said, "By God O Commander of the Faithful, he is not amongst them." Ali said, "By God, I have not lied, nor will I be accused of lying." A man came and mentioned, "We have found him O Commander of theFaithful." Ali prostrated. Whenever he receives good news during the conquests, he prostrated. He stated, "If I knew of anything better, I would have done it." Then he continued "His mark is that his hand is like an udder. It has hairs like the whiskers of a cat. Bring me his severed hand." They brought it to him and he showcased it.

[3] He mentioned this in the chapter on "those left fighting the Kharijites for safety..." from the "book of seeking the repentence of apostates and the intransigent and fighting them." Others mentioned it as well.

[4] From Khuza' (Yemen, Southern Arab). He and his companions paid allegiance to the Messenger of God (s) during the Farewell Pilgrimage. It is narrated about him that he lived in Kufa and was one of notable dignitaries. He was from the Shia of Imam Ali Ibn Abi Talib and participated in his army in several wars. He was one of the most notable companions of Hijr Ibn Adi Al-Kindi. He was martyred in the year 51 AH.

[5] Abu Al-Faraj Al-Asfahani, Al-Aghani, 17:144. Tabaqat Ibn Saad, 6:15. Ibn Qutayba, Al-Ma'ref, 291-292. He said: the head of Amro Ibn Al-Hamq was carried from Mosul to Ziyad Ibn Sumayya and Ziyad sent it to Muawiya. See also: Ibid, 554.

[6] Al-Tabari, *Tareek Al-Tabari*, 5:380.

[7] Ibid, 5:395.

[8] Ibid, 5:398.

[9] Ibid, 5:379.

[10] Ibid, 5:394.

[11] Ibid, 5:415.

[12] Ibid, 5:454-455. The two men are, Ishaq Ibn Hayawa Al-Hadrami – the man who stole the shirt of Hussain and contracted leprosy afterwards – and Ahbash Ibn Marthad Ibn Alqama Ibn Salama Al-Hadrami. The remainder of the ten are: Hani Ibn Thabeet Al-Hadrami, Salem Ibn Khaithama Al-Ju'fi, Saleh Ibn Wahab Al-Ju'fi, and Hakim

Ibn Al-Tufail Al-Sanabsi Al-Taei, those four plus the two preceding are Southern Arab from Yemen. Amro Ibn Sabeeh Al-Saidawi Al-Asadi and Raja Ibn Munqith Al-A'bdi are both from the Northern Arabs. Wakhit Ibn Ghanem and Usayd Ibn Malek, whose tribes are unknown. We note the majority of these men are from Yemen.

[13] Al-Tabari, *Tareek Al-Tabari*, 5:459

AL-ZIYARA AL-NAHIYA

[1] Ibn Tawous, *Al-Iqbal*, 573-77. Al-Majlisi, *Bihar Al-Anwar*, 22:269-74.

[2] Al-Majlisi, *Bihar Al-Anwar*, 22:274.

AL-ZIYARA AL-RAJABIA

[1] Al-Majlisi, *Bihar Al-Anwar*, 22:340-41.

[2] Al-Majlisi, *Bihar Al-Anwar*, 22:341.

A STUDY AND EXAMINATION OF THE VISITATIONS

[1] An epithet describing Sheikh Al-Tousy meaning 'Elder of the School of Thought.' – Eds.

[2] Al-Najashi, *Al-Rijal*, 67. Al-Tousy, *Al-Fahrist*, 57-58. [CITE], *Al-Kuna wa Al-Alqaab*, 1:363.

[3] Al-Tastary, *Qamous Al-Rijal*, 10:194.

[4] Al-Tahrani, *Muqadimmat Al-Tibyan*.

[5] Bahr Al-Uloom, Introduction to *Rijal Al-Sheikh Al-Tousi*, 37-38.

[6] Al-Tastari, *Qamous Al-Rijal*, 8:333-34.

[7] Literally 'the proof.' An epithet given to the Twelfth Imam Twelver Shia. –Eds.

[8] Al-Tastari, *Qamous Al-Rijal*, 8:333-34.

[9] There was another Shia term used to refer to the Twelfth Imam with respect to financial matters, which is "Al-Ghareem" – meaning creditor. This was mentioned in the book Al-Irshad by Al-Mufid: "…Muhammed Ibn Saleh stated: when my father

died and I was responsible for the affairs, my father was holding some financial obliga-tions for Al-Ghareem - meaning the Imam (a) - by others." Al-Sheikh Al-Mufid said: this was a term that the Shia would use in earlier days in reference to the Twelfth Imam out of Taqiya.

[10] Al-Qalqashandy, *Subh Al-A'sha Fi Sina't Al-Inshad*, 5:438-506. Al-Qalqashandy writes about the history of the development and circulation of the titles phenemona in government and social positions, and "its escalation to the point of exaggeration." He relays the history of this phenomenon at a time when "The Buyids of the Daylam took control. The defeated the caliphs and persecuted them. The caliphs hid and no letters came from them but what concerned governorships. Most of the time, correspondence was delegated to their ministers. This escalated until it became so that the caliph would be denoted by 'Al-Mawaqif Al-Muqadasa,' 'Al-Maqamat Al-Sharifa,' 'Al-Sira Al-Nabawiyya,' 'Al-Daar Al-Aziz,' and 'Al-Mahal Al-Mimajjad...' When circumstances became so that the caliphs were denoted by these monikers, kings and ministers were glorified by such names as 'Al-Majlis Al-'Aali,' 'Al-Hadra Al-Samiya...' The situation became so exacerbated that they began to be called 'Al-Maqam,' 'Al-Maqar,' 'Al-Janab,' 'Al-Majlis,' and the like."

[11] Ibn Tawous, *Al-Iqbal*, 712-14.

[12] Al-Majlisi, *Bihar Al-Anwar*, 22:341.

REFERENCED WORKS

Al-Ameen, Muhsen. *A'yan Al-Shia*.

Al-Asbahani, Abu Al-Faraj. *Maqaatil Al-Talibiyyin*. Beirut, n.d.

Al-Asbahani, Abu Al-Faraj. *Maqaatil Al-Talibiyyin*. Beirut, n.d.

Al-Daynouri, Ahmad ibn Dawood. *Al-Akhbar Al-Tiwal*.

Al-Daynouri, Ibn Qutayba. *Al-Imama wa Al-Siyasa*. Mustafa Babi Al-Halabi, 1968.

Al-Daynouri, Ibn Qutayba. *Al-Maaref*.

Al-Khoei, Abulqasim. *Mujam Rijaal A-Hadeeth*. Beirut, 1985.

Al-Khowarizmi, Al-Muwaffaq ibn Ahmad. *Maqtal Al-Hussain*. Qum, 1997.

Al-Majlisi. *Bihar Al-Anwar*. Beirut: Muassasat Al-Wafaa, 1991.

Al-Mas'udi, Ali ibn Hussain ibn Ali. *Murooj Al-Thahab*.

Al-Masoodi, Ali ibn Hussain. *Muruj Al-Dhahab*. Cairo, 1964.

Al-Mazandarani, Muhammad ibn Ali ibn Shahrashoub. *Manaqib Aal Abi Talib*. Najaf, n.d.

Al-Mubrad, Muhammad ibn Yazid. *Al-Kamil fi Al-Lugha wa Al-Adab*.

Al-Mufid, Muhammad ibn Muhammad. *Al-Irshad*.

Al-Najashi, Ahmad ibn Ali. *Rijal Al-Najashi*. Beirut: Daar Al-Adhwaa, n.d.

Al-Tustari, Muhammad Taqi. *Qamoos Al-Rijaal.* Qum, 1989.

Al-Yaqubi, Ahmad ibn Abi Yaqub. *Tareekh Al-Yaqubi.* Najaf, 1940.

Al-Zuhari, Muhammad ibn Saeed. *Al-Tabaqat Al-Kubra.* Beirut, 1984.

Ibn Al-Atheer, Ali ibn Muhammad. *Al-Kamil fi Al-Tareekh.* Beirut, n.d.

Ibn Tawwus, Ali ibn Musa ibn Jaafar ibn Muhammad. *Al-Luhuf fi Qatla Al-Tufoof.*

Ibrahim, Hassan. *Tareekh Al-Islam Al-Siyasi wa Al-Dini wa Al-Thaqafi wa Al-Ijtimaii.* Beirut, 1980.

www.ingramcontent.com/pod-product-compliance
Lightning Source LLC
Chambersburg PA
CBHW031042110426
42740CB00046B/294